PAPERCUTTING

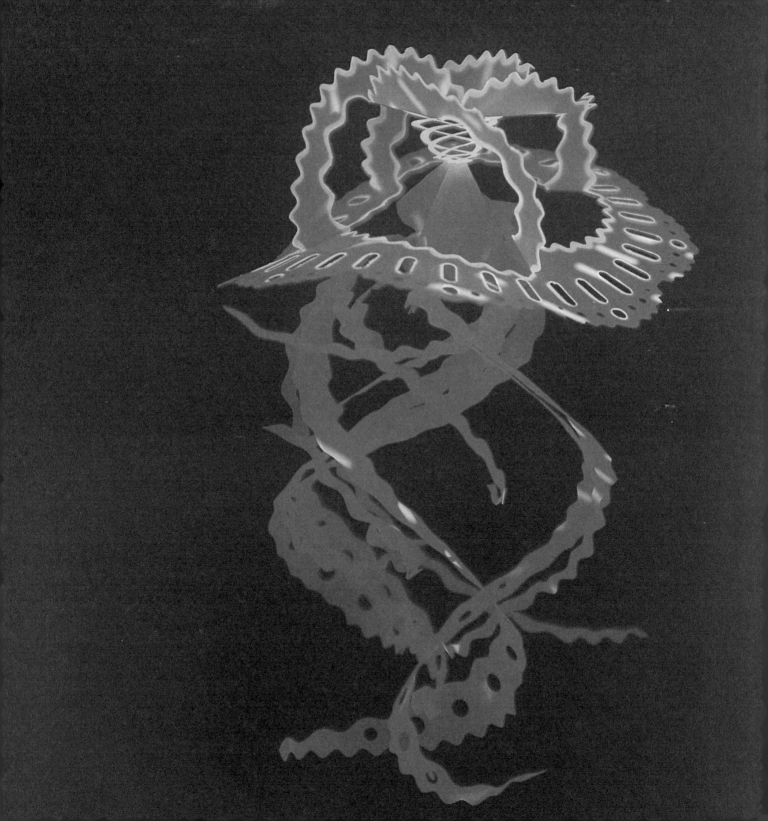

PAPERCUTTING

**GEOMETRIC
DESIGNS
INSPIRED
BY NATURE**

Patricia Moffett

SCHIFFER
PUBLISHING

4880 Lower Valley Road · Atglen, PA 19310

Authored by: Patricia Moffet

Copyright © 2019 BlueRed Press Ltd.

Library of Congress Control Number: 2019936106

Designed by Insight Design Concepts ltd.

Type set in Montserrat

ISBN: 978-0-7643-5808-1

Printed in China

Published by Schiffer Publishing, Ltd.
4880 Lower Valley Road
Atglen, PA 19310
Phone: (610) 593-1777; Fax: (610) 593-2002
E-mail: Info@schifferbooks.com
Web: www.schifferbooks.com

For our complete selection of fine books on this and related subjects, please visit our website at www.schifferbooks.com. You may also write for a free catalog.

Schiffer Publishing's titles are available at special discounts for bulk purchases for sales promotions or premiums. Special editions, including personalized covers, corporate imprints, and excerpts, can be created in large quantities for special needs. For more information, contact the publisher.

We are always looking for people to write books on new and related subjects. If you have an idea for a book, please contact us at proposals@schifferbooks.com.

Contents

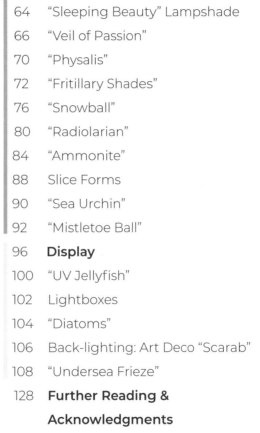

Introduction

Welcome to *Papercutting: Geometric Designs Inspired by Nature.* This fascinating theme is explored through a diverse range of papercutting techniques to learn from and experiment with.

The math behind the work

Through example pieces and projects we will explore aspects of mathematics found in nature. In particular, we will look at symmetry, the Golden Angle, and the Fibonnaci sequence.

Symmetry is at the core of many of the projects. For most people the word brings to mind mirror, or reflection, images. Symmetry is

something we've probably tried in papercutting since childhood by simply folding a piece of paper and cutting out a stick figure or perhaps a tree. Mirror symmetry is often found in creatures that need to move in forward motion. Plants show many types of symmetry, and often several kinds are present in a single flower. The examples in the papercuts on pages 18 and 19 look simple,

but study them closely and you will notice that many types of symmetry are present.

In this book we explore symmetrical forms and how to express them through papercutting. The radial symmetry of microscopic lifeforms in "Radiolarian" on pages 80–83 and the dynamic symmetries of physics in "A Murmuration of Starlings" on pages 26–29 are just two examples.

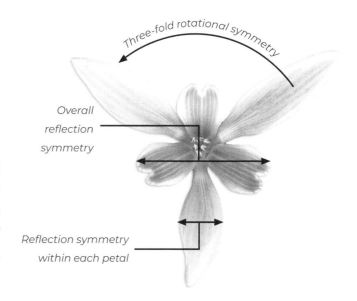

Left: Paper-cut scarab beetle with back-lighting to reveal colored wings.

When an object has both rotational symmetry and reflection symmetry it can be said to have dihedral symmetry.

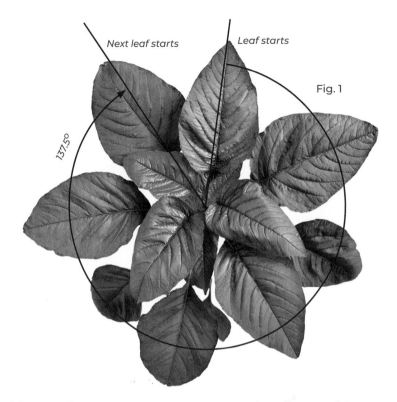

Next leaf starts

Leaf starts

Fig. 1

137.5°

The beautiful Golden Angle

Phyllotaxis, from the Greek *phýllon* meaning "leaf" and *táxis* meaning "arrangement," is the term that describes how leaves or petals grow on a plant in relation to each other. The most efficient arrangement of leaves on a stem ensures maximum exposure to the sun for each leaf, without any being overshadowed by another. This only happens if new growth is at 137.5° from the previous leaf or petal. This is often referred to as the Golden Angle and it occurs frequently in nature. If you look at a plant from above, you'll notice that new leaves are generated at points on the stem at this angle. It won't always be exact as environmental matters can have an impact, but all things being equal, 137.5° will mark the position of new growth. Furthermore, when new growth is not only at this Golden Angle but also changed in size, moved away from the center, and rotated, we get mesmerizing spirals as seen in the "Sunflower" project on pages 44–47.

The Fibonacci Sequence in plants

The Fibonacci Sequence is formed when every number in a list (after the first two) is the sum of the previous two numbers. Although the sequence had been described earlier in Indian mathematics, it became better known after Leonardo of Pisa's book of 1202, *Liber Abaci*. (He only became known as Fibonacci in 1838). Here are the first twelve numbers of his sequence: 1, 1, 2, 3, 5, 8, 13, 21, 34, 55, 89, 144. I refer to them often in this book.

Plants produce new branches in this sequence. Imagine a horizontal line across a plant—count the stems that cross it. The number usually comes from the Fibonacci Sequence. The paper-cut stand of trees on pages 50–51 is designed using this theory along with Leonardo da Vinci's rule of trees. (Also known as the area-preserving rule, this is explained on page 48.) The Fibonacci Sequence can be represented as a set of squares that fit together. If you were to run a continuous curve evenly through each square you would make what's called a Golden Spiral. See Fig. 2 below.

The Golden Spiral is an example of self symmetry, where each

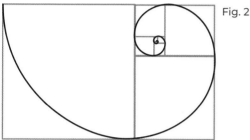

Fig. 2

section is similar, but differs through consistent application of factors of scale (dilation) and rotation. The Golden Spiral can be found in the natural world and even far beyond our world in the spiral shapes of galaxies.

Using the sequence, we'll look at aspects of symmetry from both a 2-D and 3-D viewpoint. This makes shapes that pack together in tessellations, or spring apart from—or attach to—each other with spiral structures. Mathematical themes run right through this book!

Papercutting themes

In this book the projects are grouped into three sections, followed by a final section about various ways to display the pieces. The first section, Working with a Base Sheet, starts with cutting and piercing paper, then moves on to flaps and folds coming out of a background sheet.

These simple papercutting principles are particularly developed in the fascinating constraints of kirigami, where a single sheet of paper is cut and folded so as to introduce 3-D form. The principles are simple, but the results are visually complex. The next two pieces have some fascinating applications of mathematics. Then I go on to discuss 2-D tessellations and some simple paper weaving in section two.

In the third section, I look at 3-D and modular forms, where the elements are assembled, rather than being cut to emerge from a main sheet. The skills learned in the first section are built upon, and the projects now come off the page and have a life of their own.

The forms in this section tangle up, are woven, radiate through 360°, stack with spacers, or form as cross-section slices that are locked together, and structures are formed from modular pieces.

The final section looks at the various and exciting ways that papercuts can be displayed. The pieces are developed with the final presentation being the leading component. There is a free-form piece that can be positioned in many ways for display. I also show three pieces that have lighting as their *raison d'être*—there are two lightbox pieces and one that features UV elements and black light.

I really hope that you enjoy the projects and the challenges they present, but above all I want you to develop some beautiful work from the principles described in this book. To lead into the adventure, I'll leave you with the words of D'Arcy Wentworth Thompson, the eminent Scottish biologist and mathematician.

"The perfection of mathematical beauty is such . . . that whatsoever is most beautiful and regular is also found to be most useful and excellent."

Techniques and Tips

Papercutting requires some basic equipment to get you started. If you think that it's a keeper as a hobby, there are some really handy tools it's also worth investing in—check out the Wish List.

Tools

Scalpel or Craft Knife (1): Rather than a flat scalpel, I prefer a knife that has a round handle, as it's easier to cut curves and more comfortable to hold.

Cutting Mat (2): These have fibers that close together after you've cut so you're never forced into the lines of a previous cut. Clear mats are also available for working on a lightbox.

Metal Ruler (3): This ensures you don't cut nicks out of a plastic one. The illustrated ruler opposite also has a protractor for making precise angles.

Wish List tools

If you think this hobby is a keeper, there are some really handy tools it's worth investing in.

Decoupage Scissors (4): These precision scissors rest in the open position and have fine blades. You can position them exactly where you need them and then press the spring mechanism to make the cut.

Pokey Tool (5): You'll probably find this little spear is in your hand all the time; it is a really useful tool.

Working from the back, it is also really good at bending small flaps that you can't get your finger in to. Its main purpose is poking out small circles but it is also sharp enough to cut through any cuts where the knife didn't quite make it all the way through.

Tweezers (6): Great for delicate work when embellishing and gluing. Tweezers with soft and rounded ends are really handy for curling—just grab the paper edge in the tweezers and wind the paper around the prongs.

Boning Tool (7): Popular for scoring and creasing. Personally, I find these a little thick to work with, but many people swear by them.

Scoring Stylus (8): This is my scorer of choice. It's more pen-like in the hand and I can see where the tip is going really clearly. I like the weight of it at the bottom where it's needed—it feels balanced. I also use this for tracing down and transferring patterns.

Awl or Screw Hole Punch (9): For making small holes. The awl is easy to use but does not remove the paper, just pokes a hole in it. Get one that has a tapering point so you can make holes in a range of sizes. However, if

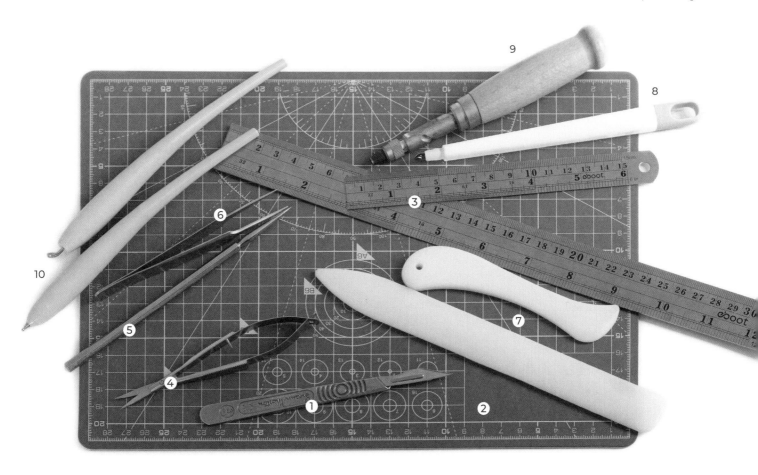

you have a pokey tool, you don't need an awl as well. A screw hole punch has a spring screw mechanism and will cut a clean circle and remove it. Most come with assorted nibs to cut different sizes. The great thing about them is, unlike a rotating or filing punch, you can make holes any distance from the edge of the material.

Embossing Tool (10): If you're working with parchment or vellum, these tools stretch the paper and the process turns those raised parts of the paper white and opaque. I have used this technique for the berries in the "Mistletoe" project on page 92. For some projects a 1.5 mm ball point embossing tool is also another handy implement to trace down with.

Materials

Paper

Transfer Paper: This is special paper that has been coated with powder and wax. It comes in black for transferring onto light paper, or in white for dark paper. It's invaluable for transferring designs—you just trace over the design you want to use, through this paper, onto your chosen material. An embossing tool or scoring stylus is great for doing this, as is a ballpoint pen that has run out of ink.

If you're in a pinch, you can make your own transfer paper by sharpening a graphite stick over some tracing paper and gently rubbing it in with a soft tissue.

Paper for Cutting: We are surrounded by paper every day. Start to notice the qualities it has—smooth/rough, shiny/matte, crisp/pulpy, opaque/transparent, printed/self-colored and you'll soon develop a habit of thinking what projects could be made from it.

Smoothness and roughness will affect how much grip a paper has. It is an important consideration for assembled projects such as a slice form, where the grip of rough watercolor paper would help the model stay together.

Shiny materials such as mirror card add interesting dimensions to work that has flaps in it, while a matte back card is a great foil for projects where other areas will light through.

Crisp paper that's had its surface ironed by hot-rollers or coated with smooth chalk will make crisp cuts. Open up a pad and flick the corner with your finger—it will make a hard snappy sound.

Pulpy paper has a soft fibery core and this can be put to good use in peeling and ripping techniques where the exposed fibers add to the effect.

The opacity or transparency of your material is important when it comes to layering or display. Vellum or parchment paper has lots of interesting qualities and when stretched becomes white and opaque.

Synthetic Papers: Made from polyethylene, these provide a versatile material and are often fully recyclable when put with HDPE plastic waste collection. These papers are tear-proof, have a degree of stretch, and are ideal for outdoor projects.

There are textured ones such as Tyvek, which have a beautiful texture when backlit—reminiscent of Japanese paper. Tyvek comes in several weights. I find the most useful is 105 gsm. It is also readily available overprinted in black or silver.

PolyArt is a smooth polyethylene paper coated with clay, which can be a little powdery to work with, but gives a texture-free finish to projects.

Glues

A good basic kit should include wet glues, tapes, and padded materials. Craft suppliers often offer a variety bag of fixings for you to try out so that you can discover which ones suit you and your projects best. In my work, just two glues seem to cover all bases.

Vellum Glue: Made to make an invisible adhesive for vellum, this glue works really well for sticking all kinds of paper together. Although on the expensive side, very little is needed and it can be applied with a cocktail stick or a pokey tool.

What I like about it is that it's quick. When sticking paper and card, the thickness of it seems to hold the two pieces together and it bonds in seconds. It is even possible to glue Tyvek with it, but it does help to leave it to become slightly tacky and then hold the pieces together for up to a minute.

Stick Glue: The other really useful glue is moist stick glue. It's usually used for covering large areas without over-wetting the paper. I prefer to use double-sided tape for that type of application, as it's a dry process. Stick glue comes into its own when sticking down really fine parts of a cut. Dig some glue out of the stick with the pokey tool, and poke it between the sheets of paper you need to stick. Give it a little squeeze then very quickly wipe away any excess.

Tapes

Clear Tape: My go-to dry fixing material: it's strong, and comes in both permanent and removable varieties. I tend to use the removable since it's quite strong. I use it whenever one-sided fixing is needed that's not just tacking something into position.

Masking Tape: For tacking into position, I find very low tack masking tape (often purple in color) is the best to use. Paper can be delicate, and any tape that's not staying put must be able to be removed easily without damage or leaving a residue.

Double-sided Tape: Used to fix pieces of paper together. The tape itself needs to be really thin, so as not to create a bump, but the backing strips are best when they're thick and easy to separate. As the bond is permanent, it's important to be able to see the position clearly. Some come with a red backing strip that makes this easy, so you're more likely to get it right the first time. Get a roll each of 3 mm and 6 mm widths.

Foam Tape: Used to create space between elements such as in the "Ammonite" project on page 84. It's double-sided tape that has a 1 mm layer of foam between the adhesive. It can be used on top of itself for more depth, but make sure to remove the backing strip of each piece before you add another layer—after all, the tape is designed not to stick to that strip.

Techniques

Templates

A number of templates are provided in this book so that you can make the stunning projects yourself. You can either trace them or scan them to copy onto your chosen paper. Cut along the black lines and fold or score along the pink dotted lines. The beauty of scanning is that the pieces can be scaled up or down in size according to your needs and quickly printed off in the quantity you require.

Cutting fine detail

In tiny areas it's sometimes tricky to make a one-time deep cut that has sufficient depth. This means that you may have to cut these out over several passes. The areas can be weeded easily by pressing your knife blade in (or a pokey tool), and using it to pull the paper away.

Working your curves

Cut lines that run in a similar direction at the same time. Rotate the cutting mat until the angle is comfortable to cut, then rotate again for the next direction.

Clean as you go

If the piece you're working on has large areas that are discarded, it can be much easier to work if you chop them away a bit at a time.

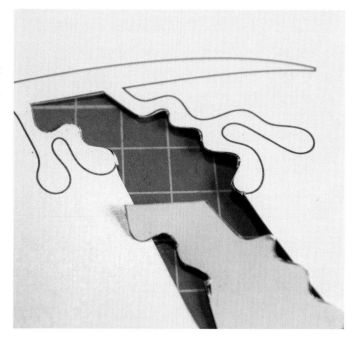

Carving paper

Paper can be carved so that the rough inner fibers are exposed. This gives a suede-like appearance which contrasts nicely with the smooth surface. It also, of course, makes the paper thinner, resulting in interesting effects when used with a background light source. A lightbox makes it easier to see score lines and the effect of removing layers. Score around the shape, then gently pick at an edge. Work that layer back to get a crest of paper and pull away with tweezers. In the photograph you can see the difference that removing a further layer has made.

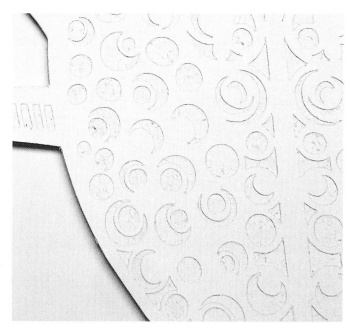

Scoring

Scoring is when only the very top layer of paper is cut or scored so as to make the fold sharp and precise. In many ways, scoring is trickier than cutting—too much pressure when cutting means that the piece is still cut, too little and you can cut it again.

The pressure you use and the resulting depth when scoring is important; see the photograph below. Sometimes you will need to score on the side of the paper that you don't have guide lines on. If you don't have a lightbox to be able to see these guide lines through the paper, these marks will need to be transferred.

The easiest way to do this is to make little nicks through the paper with your blade at the start and finish points on the annotated side. These will be barely visible from the side you need to score, but you'll find your blade rests nicely in them. Run a ruler between both the nicks and score.

Left: The score line on the left is too deep and the layers of card have started to separate. The one in the middle is too shallow and there are bumps in the fold. The one on the right is correct—it is a crisp line without breaking the integrity of the card. Practice the amount of pressure needed.

Folding away

Most folds wider than 1 cm benefit from being scored first.

Any folding you do doesn't have to be a one-time action. Start by gently breaking the fold line then work up to good sharp pinch—stop anywhere in between once you've achieved the effect you like.

When folding an area that's in the middle of a papercut, use any openings you can to get your fingers nearer. If that's impossible then use a toothpick or a pokey tool.

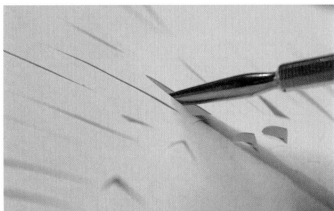

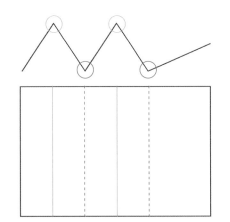

Mountain

Valley

Working with a
Base Sheet

Flaps and Piercings

The artworks in this book develop in complexity, with new aspects of papercutting being factored in along the journey. This first section deals with taking a sheet of paper and looking at what happens when you slice it, cut a hole in it, or bend a bit of it back.

Stylizing shapes to emphasize form

In 1856 Owen Jones published *The Grammar of Ornament*, in which he displays the "general principles in the arrangement of form and colour in architecture and the decorative arts." It is a seminal work on pattern and design. In it he notes that his original sources were depicted with shading to show naturalistic form and were "highly illuminated." He goes on to explain his decision to reproduce his versions of the patterns by using two colors only: that the character of each plant can be made more apparent by representing it in diagrammatic form. Then he invites the reader to explore the same principles. This process of capturing form as a silhouette in the source material is perfect for exploring as a papercut.

There is so much to look for in this apparently simple illustration from his classic volume. In the introduction I briefly discussed and showed the relevance of the Fibonacci Sequence and the resulting Golden Spiral, and here in this floral design are two examples interwoven in one illustration.Using the diagrams overleaf, study and name the forms of the symmetries of each part of Jones' illustration. Get into the habit of breaking down and analysing the forms of the world around you.

This first example

In this very first piece, we're considering a sheet of paper, what's there and, just as importantly, what's missing from it.

The examples on pages 22 and 23 use the blue front sheet of paper to make the "bones" of the design in the same way that Owen Jones uses the green color in his example. That green is cut as a positive shape, and runs as a single joined-up piece.

The red elements in Jones's piece are cut as negative shapes. That is, they are missing from the cream sheet of paper. Cutting and attaching these pieces as positive shapes would be very tricky. As we have, in effect, made windows out of them we can see the color of any paper behind them. To add interest, different colors of paper can be stuck behind these windows.

Opposite: A reproduction from The Grammar of Ornament, *Owen Jones, 1856. In it Jones presents an array of flower designs collected from medieval illuminated manuscripts.*

Overall the design has symmetry through rotating (not reflecting) through 180°. This symmetry is also found in the face card portraits on playing cards.

Symmetry in its many forms is absolutely central to this book. In the introduction it was noted that symmetry means much more than the simple mirror symmetry that the word often conjures up. Later on we'll be looking at symmetries of motion and the intriguing spontaneous order of self-organizing symmetries, but we're going to start here with the basic orders, and use them to tune in to the illustration on page 21.

Root object

Two-fold symmetry through 180°

Reflection symmetry through vertical 180°

Reflection symmetry through vertical 180° —note, no rotational symmetry

Reflection symmetry and rotational symmetry three-fold through 120° —if an object has both reflection and rotational symmetry, it can be described as having dihedral symmetry

Reflection symmetry through horizontal 180°

Dihedral symmetry

Dihedral symmetry

Mapping Forces

As a starting point I took a look at the marks from Leonardo Da Vinci's amazing drawings of natural forces.

My favorite is this marvellous study of pouring water. It involves the energetic mapping of forces—the swirls and dashes of air and liquid, and fast liquid moving through slow. In particular, I love the force of the pouring water causing the rising mounds of spouts and bubbles. Everything is mixed up, yet it's all clear—concentric circles and spirals of turbulence. This is the 3-D world mapped in 2-D, onto paper, in early 16th-century Renaissance Italy.

Da Vinci's scratchy lines made me think of cuts in paper, and the bubbles are like piercings. What would happen if you transcribed these drawn lines into cuts on paper, then looked at the shapes and tensions they formed? This is essentially an exercise in taking a source that has transcribed 3-D and movement to a flat drawing, then cutting these 2-D marks to see what the resulting forms are.

To hold the shape together, I decided to give the whole design three-fold symmetry. I find the resulting tensions in the middle of the piece interesting to look at—the spirals contrarotating against the marks representing the little rising mounds. I then picked away at these shapes to see how much lift each could take. The spirals bob up delightfully and the tight crescents in the mounds, when pushed to fold as far as they are able, make a nice texture.

The drawn dashes of concentric circles, when pulled in opposite directions, give a fair amount of depth and make interesting shadows. I attempted to stretch the bubble holes with a bradawl (an awl with a chisel edge). I'd imagined this would make the bubbles weaker; instead the resulting curled rim of the circle made the structure more rigid.

"A Murmuration of Starlings"

When I lived for many years overlooking the promenade in the town of Aberystwyth, Wales, it was a delight to witness the beautiful displays of starlings in the winter months as they came to roost under the pier every evening. This flock is called a murmuration.

Mesmerizing shapes, and the dark dense areas switching direction in the evening sky suddenly to spread out like a firework, seem so mysteriously created. What are the forces at work behind these forms? We often think of symmetry as having the fixed qualities of reflection, rotation, etc., but there are also symmetries of curvature in motion. This self-organizing symmetry is studied in the fields of turbulence and chaos theory.

The design of the cut

When you observe a murmuration, there is both similarity in the shapes the birds make, as well as an overall change in that shape, which moves constantly through the clusters.

We see this often in nature—things that are seemingly random yet have elements of similarity. It is a product of more than one influence on a group of elements. We'll see it again in the inspirational picture for "Falling Water" (see page 35), and later in the "Honeycomb" project (page 58). It's called self-organizing symmetry.

I have suggested this in the papercut by using just three basic shapes of flying starlings. This means there is similarity throughout the piece and these constant elements act as a device to help you notice the differences. The limited variation of shapes highlights the shifts in scale and direction.

As you can see in the photograph, the starlings make vortex shapes as they twist and climb through the air together, then quickly explode into separate clouds. My papercut is a stylized version of this, this sudden transition shape from vortex to splitting off, that I chose for the cut.

The choice of materials

This papercut was made from vellum and backed with black card. Lighting then provides additional tone through shadows. As these shadows are a product of the flaps in the cuts, they function almost like in-between frames in an animation and add to the flickering effect of the birds in movement.

Overleaf: "A Murmuration of Starlings" papercut, vellum over black card.

Right: Each evening between October and March tens of thousands of starlings fly in the sky above the town of Aberystwyth before settling to roost for the night on the cast iron legs of the Victorian seaside pier.

"Butterfly"

Butterflies within a butterfly! As we have seen in "A Murmuration of Starlings," flaps in papercutting throw out exciting possibilities for lighting and shadows.

Reflection symmetries reflected symmetrically

When cut in mirror card the variety in the angles and position of the flaps will pick up reflections of all the different colors in the surrounding room.

This is a simple project but very pleasing to look at. It looks great simply hung on a wall, but back it with a contrasting color and it would make a delightful greeting card, or repeat the cut on a long strip of card to make a wrap-around lampshade.

The shapes have both open and tight curves along with runs of straight edges, making this a great practice piece for new paper crafters, as well as being ideal for the more experienced to warm up on.

Step-by-step

Making this project is really simple:

1. Transfer the design at the size you'd like, onto the material of your choice.

2. Cut the solid black lines and score the pink lines.

3. Push the wings out from the back.

4. As always, techniques and methods can be found on pages 14–17.

Kirigami—"Falling Water"

This kirigami piece is inspired by the repeating shapes in a cascade. The falling curtains of water in this beautiful waterfall exhibit some subtle regularity in their distance and spacing. There are common widths, symmetrical smaller falls on either side of bigger ones, and rows that are of similar heights.

In his book *Symmetry: The Ordering Principle*, David Wade explains how forces in nature work against each other to make a self-organizing symmetry. He points out that rivers will both shape, and be shaped by, the landscape they flow through.

We can see this happening in the cascade pictured here. The bedrock is made up of distinct layers. These layers are tidal bundles: deposits on the sea bed of varying thicknesses corresponding to ancient tides. Every so often there is a wide shelf—these occur below the tallest falls. Although there is variation, overall the rows of falls get deeper and deeper, until the resulting increased force is enough to break off a layer of rock. The flow then crosses the horizontal shelf before starting another cycle.

This all seems to be just the river shaping the rock, but the nature of the rock itself plays a part. On the far left of the picture you can see that some of the rock is undercut. In spite of the force of the water above, softer rock below has eroded first. The orientation of the rock—how it lies—is also a factor in helping to dictate how it breaks under the force of the water. The shape of the break then affects the force of the water and so on—and right there we have our reciprocal cycle. The way that the subsequent rows of the falls appear to grow down and out from the ones before them made this an interesting subject for kirigami.

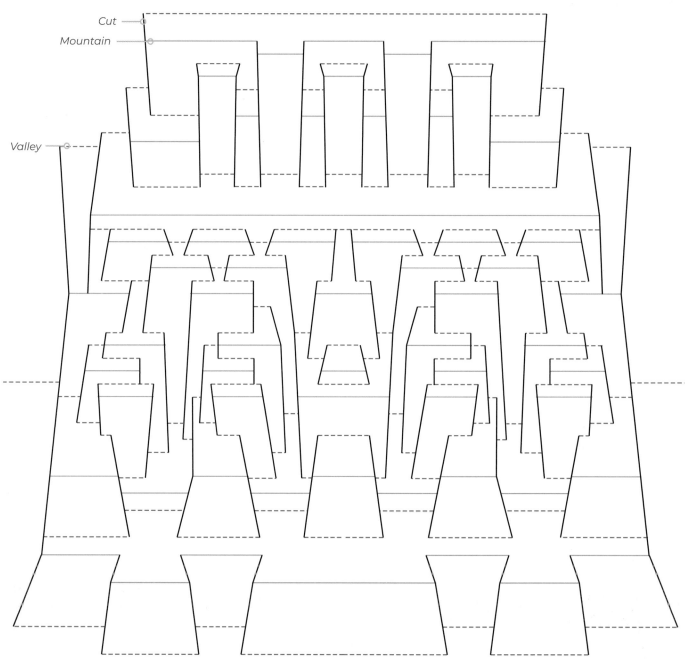

Cut

Mountain

Valley

Basic principles of kirigami

The word *kirigami* is derived from the Japanese words *kiri* (cut) and *kami* (paper). Unlike origami, in which paper is folded, with kirigami paper is cut and usually, in simple geometric work, folded at right angles to the cuts.

It can be quite a tricky thing to work out how to even start a design. When you look at a template from an expert such as Guy Petzall (ullagami.com), it is so well developed and refined that the starting point is often no longer visible.

Above: Front view of the work in progress showing the shapes and volumes that are not always obvious from the front.

Here is my personal golden kirigami mantra:

"As above, so below."

And the dividing point of the two is the central crease. Looking at **Fig. 1**, the distance (B) that C drops below the central crease, is the same length that the supporting tab (A) will be. C can vary, but A must always equal B—as above, so below.

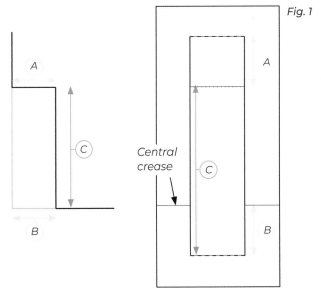

Right: This side view is the one that really makes it clear—in order for all the folds to be right angles, it shows why A must equal B.

These two pages illustrate the principles of designing kirigami, followed by a simple example for you to make. After this, you should be equipped to design your own project. Here are some isometric projections of how it works.

Fig. 1 shows a single item projecting from the folded background. The projection length A, remember, must be the same as B. The length of the cuts is C+A, but the actual height of the projection is C.

Fig. 2 This shows a generation—a new single item grown from the original. Notice that the old fold at the bottom is now counted as the central crease for the new generation. This distance from this new central crease to the bottom of C, determines the depth of A.

Fig. 3 This looks complicated as there are cuts of two lengths, but follow the "as above, so below" principle and it will fall into place. The key is that any new generations wider than the original item have their supporting tabs measured back to the central crease directly above it.

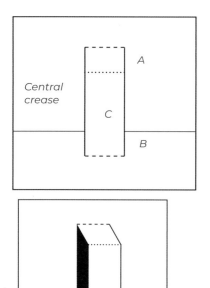

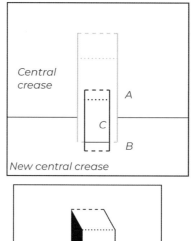

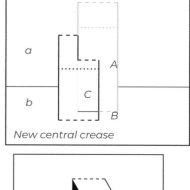

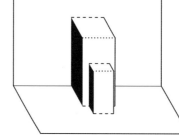

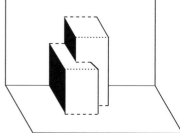

How the volumes develop

Kirigami can also be worked with the central tab running vertically, and parts A and C then becoming right and left sides of the item.

As a beginner, though, it's simpler to work with the central crease horizontal. Working this way it's easy to visualize the items are characters on a stage, standing in front of each other. The tabs act like characters at the back with their arms outstretched to support those standing in front of them in descending heights.

Kirigami Project

Try out the theory with this great starter waterfall project—a simple kirigami project to get you familiar with the principles of the discipline.

This design is based on a waterfall in a gorge. A sense of harmony is achieved by enlarging the scale of the items according to the Fibonacci Sequence, which we looked at on page 8 in the Introduction.

How to make it

Making this project is really simple as there are no tight folds to worry about.

Transfer the design at the size you'd like on to the material of your choice. Surprisingly, you don't need thick card for kirigami, in fact if it's too thick then the folds won't be crisp enough.

Paper that's around 100 gsm will be perfect.

The back is the side of the paper that has the transferred design on it.

Step-by-step

1. Score all the mountain folds, the dashed lines, from the back.
2. Score all the valley folds, the dotted lines, from the front.
   If you have a lightbox this will be easy. If you don't have a lightbox, then the easiest thing to do is to make little nicks at each end of the line from the back with your scalpel or knife, turn the sheet over, and score between them on the front.
3. Cut the solid black lines.
4. Start by folding the central crease.
5. From the back start to fold all the mountain folds.
6. From the front start to fold all the valley folds.
7. Don't expect to get crisp folds right away when working a piece; concentrate on easing-in the folds and continue to work around and around until the folds are knife sharp. As always, techniques and methods can be found on pages 14–17.

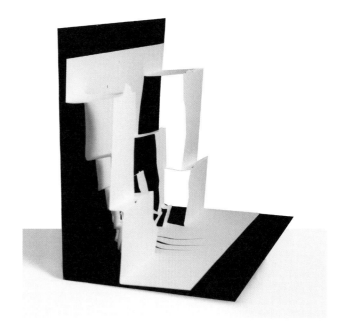

Above: Side view of the work in progress showing the shapes and volumes that are not always obvious from the front.

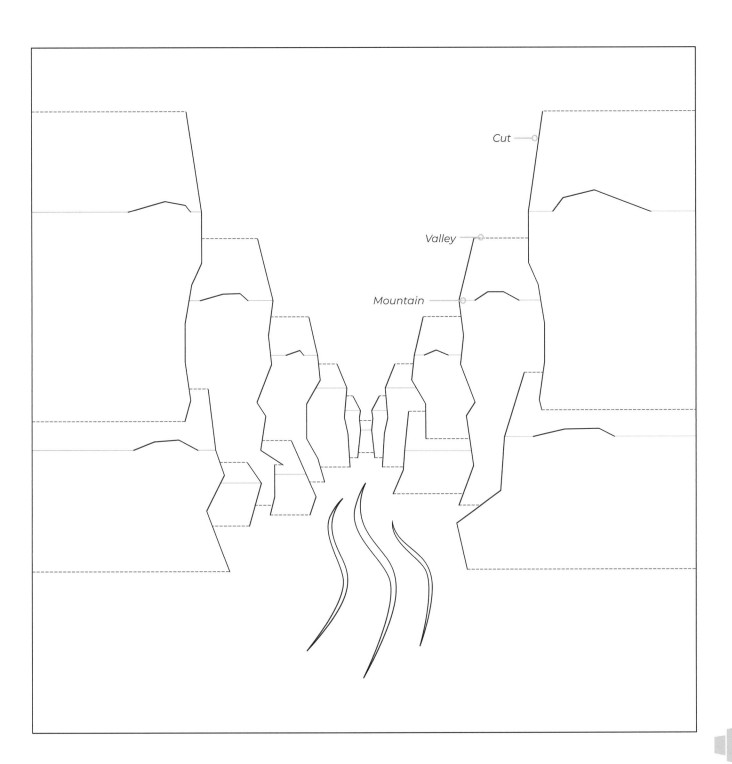

Geometry, Phyllotaxis, and Fibonacci

In this section I will expand on what I have already explained about basic expressions of symmetry, and will add some new factors in.

Rotational symmetry plus

At the beginning of this book we looked at the Golden Angle of 137.5º and how it's found in phyllotaxis, or the arrangement of leaves or petals. We discussed reflection and rotation symmetries where elements were either reflected through a central line, or rotated at equal angles through a central point. Now let's consider more complex types of rotational symmetry and how the Fibonacci Sequence is expressed in them.

Rotational symmetry describes the rotation of elements around a (usually) central point at a given angle. But this can be combined with a factor of size, or dilation. The resulting symmetry provides us with the mesmerizing spiral form found in nature. The spiral of a nautilus shell is a well known symmetry of dilation and rotation combined, with each new section being an enlargement of the previous one at a constant angle from the center.

Above: This nautilus shell has self-similar symmetry: each section is a scaled and rotated version of the previous one and all the others.

Left: Geometric arrangement of the leaves, seen from above. Each leaf gets optimum exposure to light.

Above: The lines map the three lines of spirals found in a pineapple.

Spirals and Fibonacci numbers

Fibonacci numbers are important because they are the mathematical representation of growth patterns in nature. The numbers themselves aren't driving the patterns, they merely represent what's happing during growth. They are the result of what happens when a plant, such as a tree, divides in the most efficient way, while resting alternate branches from division. You can find this mapped on page 49.

When several spirals are generated in a plant, such as in a pine cone, or in the pineapple on the left, the number of spirals is almost always a number in the Fibonacci Sequence. In pineapples, three sets of spirals can be traced. There are gentle curving, and also medium curving spirals running in the opposite direction, plus a steep set of spirals. The number of each set of spirals always corresponds to three consecutive numbers in the Fibonacci Sequence.

The following pages contain an explanation of the "Sunflower" project, and this time the papercut includes two types of symmetry:

- Rotational symmetry through the the Golden Angle of 137.5° shown in the arrangement of the petals.
- Rotational symmetry plus dilation for the seeds. The resulting spirals number 13 counterclockwise and 34 clockwise. The angle that is used to generate the next seed ensures that the number of spirals will be from the Fibonacci Sequence.

43

"Sunflower"

Golden Fibonacci fun in flower form

This is another project that uses flaps to great effect to provide light and shade. As well as replicating the form of the petals and seeds of a sunflower, the flaps allow effective use to be made of a backing sheet and the fall of shadow.

Before you start

Consider the materials you'll use.

I'm a big fan of pads of scrapbooking card that you can pick up in crafting superstores. It tends to cut crisply and comes in generous 12 x 12-inch pads. In particular I like using the type that has different colors printed on each side. They are often sold in packs of either deep colors or pastel combinations.

Play around before you start and ask yourself a couple of questions: What backing card will enhance the cut?

Should I consider using different colors to back different parts?

Which will be my front-facing color, and which will be revealed by forming the make?

How does the reflection of the back color of the sheet get picked up on the front?

To make it

This papercut is very straightforward to make. There is no need to score before bending as the elements aren't very wide and so will bend readily.

I found the best tool for bending the petals is a pokey tool (see page 10). Simply rest it at the edge of the crease and rock it forward to make the bend. It's worth working around the make several times to really get a lot of lift—the more lift each flap has, the more of the background color will be revealed, to a great graphic effect.

Step-by-step

1. Transfer the design at the size you want onto your chosen material.
2. Cut the black lines.
3. Bend all the elements apart from the triangles in the very center.
4. For the triangles in the center, clasp the tips gently with tweezers and roll them back until they form a curl.
5. Fix your backing materials and you're done!

Cut around the black lines, and
mountain fold each one at the base.

Cut

"Trees in Winter"

This piece considers only the patterns and geometry seen when the tree is viewed as a flattened, silhouette form. Additional aspects of the math used will be explored in later chapters.

Leonardo's rule

Leonardo da Vinci proposed that the thickness of a tree at any given point is constant. If two branches form from a trunk, then the combined area of them in cross section is equal to that of the trunk they branched from.

But just how and why does the tree divide into branches? Does each branch divide into two as mirror symmetry?

The answer is that the branching pattern follows the Fibonacci Sequence.

Using this theory, but adding a curve to each of the lengths for interest, I made a papercut of nine trees. The design follows the rules of Fig. 1 strictly, but, by varying the length of the sections and angles of the joins, an interesting set of variations is produced.

The fine branches of the smaller trees continue out toward the trunks of their larger neighbors. This gives rigidity and adds to the overall stability of the design—useful as the trees need to stand up by their trunks alone. The finished design can be displayed flat or curled into a grove.

Fig. 1: The number of bars in each row follows the Fibonacci Sequence. The width of each bar is the width of the inital trunk divided by the Fibonacci number for that row.

Fig. 2: The overall shape of each branching plant form is determined by the distance between the rows and the angle at the point they join.

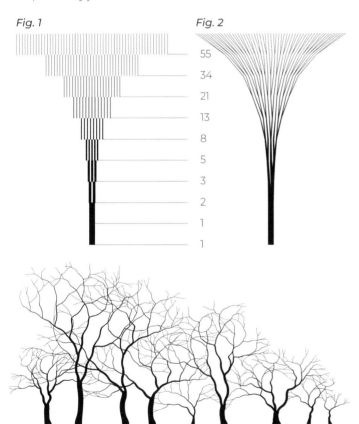

Fig. 1

Fig. 2

55

34

21

13

8

5

3

2

1

1

Opposite: Notice how as the thickness of the branches tapers, the number of branches increases.

Right: The piece can be curled around so that the line of trees resembles a grove. The tangling shapes and shadows are fascinating.

Above: A second set of trees in a medium with different qualities, in this case vellum. Combining the two sets makes for a fascinating interplay of transmitted light through the paper and a complex pattern of cast shadows.

Right: Dramatically lit, the silhouettes of the trees throw shadows across the ground. At a larger scale this would be brilliant for a stage set.

"Trees in Winter"

Tessellations and
2-D Weaving

Tessellations and 2-D Weaving

An array is the term for when similar shapes are arranged in an ordered way over an area. If shapes fit together to form a pattern with no space between them then they are said to tessellate. The simple shapes of bricks in a wall tessellate, but so do the more elaborate patterns found in Islamic tiling. These patterns comprise many shapes all designed to fit together as a regular pattern.

Paper weaving is when two layered pieces of paper have elements in one that can be pulled through slots in the other.

I often start my designs from tessellations so that there is a background structure holding the composition together, then expand certain areas to give rhythm. The "Lichen Rosette" and "Honeycomb" projects are based around symmetries of array and tessellation. The composition of "Lichen Rosette" starts off with an array of circles, some of which are merged to create tessellating shapes, and other circles are expanded to give variety and rhythm to the composition. In "Honeycomb," tiles are formed from tessellating hexagons and the resulting tile itself also tessellates to form larger compositions.

The inspiration for the lichen piece comes from winter walks near my home village in Snowdonia. Carpets of bright green lichen cover slabs of gray slate, and the stone walls are completely upholstered and re-colored by mosses and lichens. I love the way the circular patches of plants grow and merge into each other. It's fascinating how the repeating forms in each circle increase in size the nearer the border they are.

As mentioned above, "Lichen Rosette" has an underlying grid comprising an array of circles which is a simple grid with the circles touching top, bottom, and sides. Looking at this grid in Fig. 1 you'll notice that It's possible to bridge the circles and form interlocking dumbell shapes that are shown as yellow and blue shapes. The area where these shapes overlap is green.

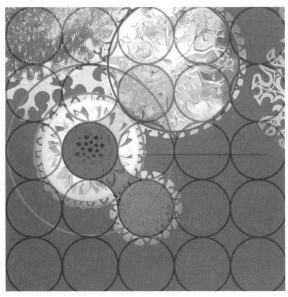

Fig. 1: A grid of gray circles forms the basic array from which interlocking dumbell shapes are drawn. Concentric circles around some of the grid circles are used to add dynamism and interest—this interplay of the regular and irregular emulates self-organizing symmetries.

If these shapes were made of paper, then the green circle would comprise two layers. This overlap of circles makes an ideal opportunity for some weaving where flaps in the bottom shape are pulled through slots on the uppermost one.

Going back to Fig. 1, you'll notice expanded circles, shown as blue and orange key lines. These, for the sake of composition and fit, relate to either center points (blue key line) or edges (orange key line) of the gray circles in the grid.

Using this layout of circles and the spaces between them, several species of lichen have been represented in paper and card form. See pages 52–53.

Two materials are used to make the project—mirror card and vellum. These have opposing qualities that I really like to see working together: the mirror card reflects light and is opaque, while the vellum seems to hold light within itself and is translucent. When vellum is placed over the mirror card, the vellum transmits the light reflected from the card, resulting in a papercut that appears to glow from within. Both materials cut beautifully, but mirror card also responds really well to being scored, giving an embossed look to the work.

For the woven elements I've worked both the vellum and the mirror card through each other.

As circles don't naturally pack together without including the space between them as part of the pattern, the more familiar tessellations use straight lines. The "Honeycomb" project is based on the hexagonal wax cells that bees make to store honey. Hexagons can be subdivided into six equilateral triangles.

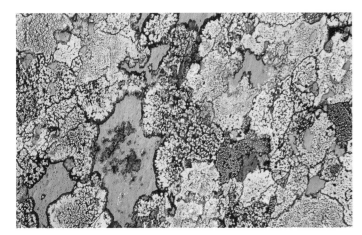

Circles of the bright green lichen rhizocarpon geographicum growing into each other on this slate slab on top of the exposed mountain Moelwyn Bach. Its common name is map lichen, and it does indeed look like a map—maybe of some lush and tropical islands, or perhaps paddy fields, or the Amazon basin.

Detail of one of the rosettes.

Triangles

An equilateral triangle is made from three 60° angles, and a tessellating grid of these triangles forms the basis of our hexagons of honeycomb.

Grids of equilateral triangles are often the base grids in the fascinating patterns of Islamic tile design. Here on the right are some examples that have this triangle as a base. For more complicated grids that use multiple shapes as their base, check out Penrose tiling, named after mathematician Roger Penrose. These are tessellating forms that develop without becoming areas of repeats. They are self-similar, and appear to grow from a point, and sequences are often repeated at larger scales. Several tile shapes can be used and and many are derived from golden ratio divisions of a pentangle. For my design I have used two classic Penrose shapes, the 36° and the 72° rhombi.

This papercut is inspired by the display of surface curve reflections on water and I used the Penrose method of tessellation to design it. I started off by using two rhombus tiles to make the pattern. A design using lines is made for each type of tile shape, making sure that the lines touch somewhere when the two types of tile are next to each other. The tiles are then fitted together. This forms a connecting pattern of lines, so when you take away the borders of the tiles themselves, you are left with the paths that make this beautiful woven pattern on the right.

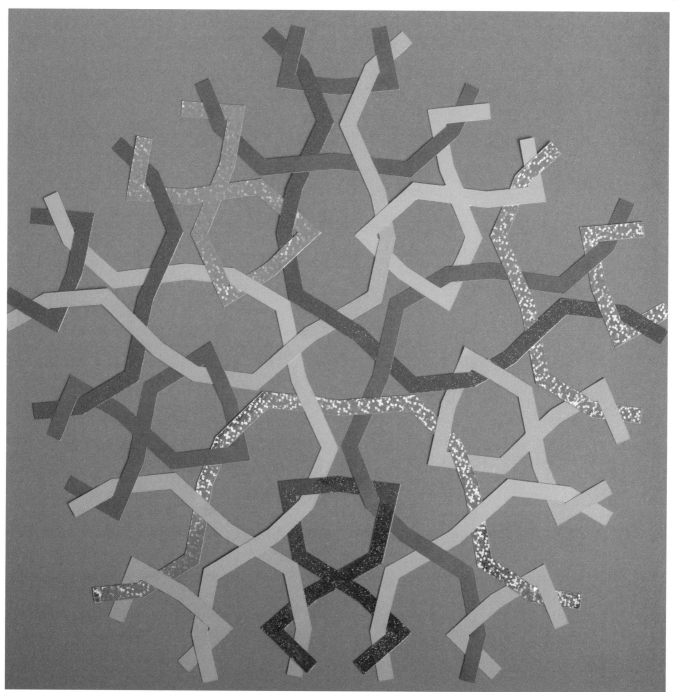

"Honeycomb"

Self organizing symmetry over tessellating tiles

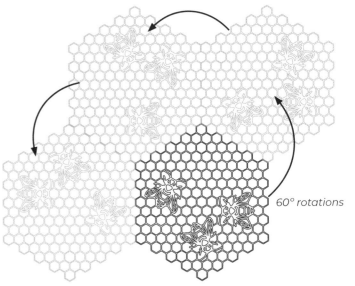

60° rotations

Looking at photographs of bees on a honeycomb, I was struck by the common angles the bees made on the grid.

The reason is probably one of pure comfort as each bee straddles the honeycomb for a firm position to settle.

This piece would make a pretty summer window screen, cutting down the light levels to provide some gentle shade, while at the same time casting some fascinating shadows.

Step-by-step

1. Measure the area you'd like to cover with the papercut and scale the template accordingly.
2. Carefully cut out your tiles using the template on page 59.
3. Align the tiles as shown in the diagram on the right—rotate the tiles regularly as you work to break up the repeat.
4. Add tiny dots of PVA to secure the tiles in position.

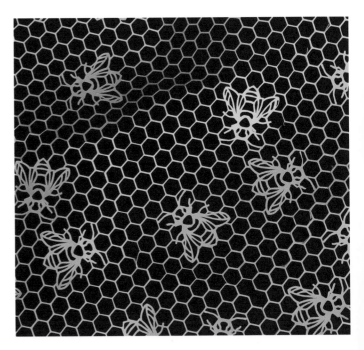

Cut

Assembling
3-D Forms

Assembling 3-D Forms

In this section we'll look at how to plan, cut, and assemble various 3-D forms. As these pieces are moving out of a flat background to form shapes with volume, the materials used have to have the right qualities for each project.

The first two pieces are tangle-form structures. This is where the spiral elements of the design serve to catch and attach pieces to each other, or give spring and volume to the work. The two pieces have contrasting themes: the card the "Sleeping Beauty" Lampshade (right) is made from gives resistance between the pieces and so contributes to its volume. The "Veil of Passion" project (see page 66) is soft enough to allow the spiral tendrils to tangle and attach to each other, as well as letting the finished piece drape. The forms of the pieces are different too: "Sleeping Beauty" has rotational symmetry, while the "Veil" is constructed in a way that in itself replicates the self-organizing symmetry I discussed earlier.

Next, for my "Physalis" project (page 70), I describe 3-D weaving, both as a regular geometric shape and more free-form, enjoying the springy delights of notched vellum.

Form is also expressed in two ways with layers of flat paper—by spacing out a stack of flat sheets or by rotating them around a central axis, such as in "Mistletoe Ball" (page 92).

In the following pages there are projects and examples that make structures from assembled identical parts. They are woven together in the "Snowball," slotted together in the "Urchin," or constructed, slotted, or glued in "Mistletoe Ball."

"Sleeping Beauty" Lampshade

This project started out as a response to a gift of a very pretty lightbulb. I wanted to design a shading device that still allowed the bulb to be seen. I chose a brambly, deep red card, backed with purple. The two colors are close in tone, with a slight shift in the hues, giving the effect of richness rather than contrast. The twining of the briar around the light reminds me of Sleeping Beauty.

Step-by-step

1. Measure the diameter of the light fitting itself—not the separator ring.
2. Scale the template up or down, until the hole in the middle has a diameter about 1 mm more than the light fitting, but less than that of the separator ring.
3. Cut around all the black lines of the template (right).
4. Unscrew the bottom part of the light fitting and remove the separator ring.
5. Carefully work the wired fitting through the hole in the middle of the cut.
6. Replace the ring and the lower part.
7. Arrange the papercut by pulling the parts down and around to form a pleasing form—the spirals and thorns enable it to hook and attach to itself. Make sure the paper *does not* touch the bulb at any point.
8. The cuts can be repeated and stacked on top of each other.

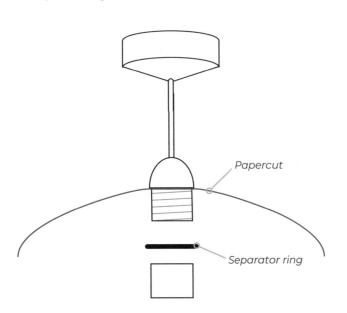

Papercut

Separator ring

Cut

"Veil of Passion"

Vines, such as the passionflower, or *Passiflora*, are able to cling and climb when their tendrils hook around the frame of a host plant or structure.

This example has been cut from white and silver Tyvek, a polyester paper that's waterproof and will not rip or tear. This means it would make an beautiful and original outdoor decoration for a wedding, no matter how the weather turns out.

Step-by-step

1. Cut out the template on page 68. You'll need at least twenty.
2. Score and fold along the indicated lines.
3. On the flowers, curl the anthers up away from the petals.

Assembly

This project can be made as either a garland or a veil. To assemble simply entwine the pieces in a random places to create the desired effect. If you are cutting from a material that has a printed metallic side then it will catch more light if you use a mountain fold on the metallic side. The veil will twist and turn around in all directions as it catches the breeze.

"Physalis"

Weaving paper is a particularly popular pastime in Denmark and Norway. Projects can range from simple hearts to complex 3-D forms.

I was interested in developing a woven project that had both informal weaving and tension in the weaving itself that would be enough to hold it together without glue.

The physalis subject came about from a long-held fascination in the contrast between their dry slightly spiky cages and the succulent orange berry they hold within. That tantalizing glimpse of striking orange color through the dry shell is inspiration in itself.

Each physalis is made up of five separate pieces. Note that even the berry is part of the cutout and will be hand colored. Each berry and cage piece is folded along the center in opposite directions. The five pieces are woven together free style, trapping the berry in the middle. Notches in the weaving pieces and the slots provide additional grip; this is important if you are using a slippery medium, such as vellum, as I have here.

When devloping and designing woven projects, consider the qualities of the medium you'll be using, and whether they'll help or hinder the design. Factors to consider include spring and bounce when folded, the grip or

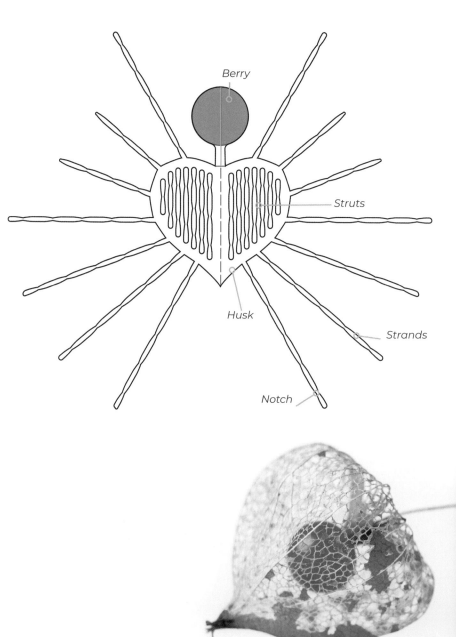

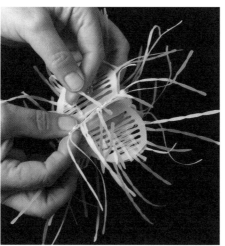

Color the berry, then fold and glue the five berry parts together. Fold the husks along the mountain fold line.

Tuck the berry down into one of the husk sections. Using the short strands weave through the struts in the husks.

Once the husk's struts are firm, the longer strands weave between the struts to form the outside of the husk cage.

slippery nature of the material, and its transparency to hide or reveal the woven elements through each other.

The next two projects, "Fritillary Shades" and "Snowball," use formal geometrical weaving to make crisp, solid structures. The former is made as two mirror pieces that interweave like a wicker basket, while the latter is made from three identical pieces that weave through each other.

In the first project, the "Fritillary Shades," securing the first three spokes in each section makes a sturdy frame to weave the remaining spokes into. The ripples on the spokes, as well as emulating the soft patchworks and checkers in the natural flowers, act to add resistance and grip the spokes in position.

In the "Snowball" project, the ball itself is soft and mobile until the semicircles are folded down. This snaps and locks the ball into a solid structure.

Both projects need an adhesive medium to either secure the initial spokes or to close the woven loops.

"Fritillary Shades"

The delightful snake's head fritillary can be seen nodding in grassy meadows in early summer. The checkerboard pattern on the petals is striking and ranges through many shades of dusky pinks and purples.

Step-by-step

1. Cut out two layers using the template on page 74. And remember to flip over the template for the second cutout so the spokes rotate in the opposite direction.

2. Place the two petal parts over each other, making sure the arms of each piece rotate in opposite directions. Follow the diagram on the right.

3. Note that there are three lengths of arms, and the easiest way to check the placement is to have the short pieces mirroring each other.

4. Then, make sure they're offset so that you can see the spokes of the bottom piece of paper between the spokes of the top one.

5. Glue the two central disks together.

6. Lightly number the arms with a pencil, as shown in the diagrams and photos.

Template

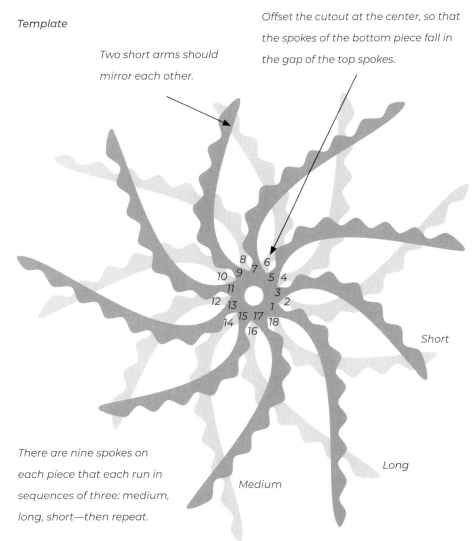

Two short arms should mirror each other.

Offset the cutout at the center, so that the spokes of the bottom piece fall in the gap of the top spokes.

Short

Long

Medium

There are nine spokes on each piece that each run in sequences of three: medium, long, short—then repeat.

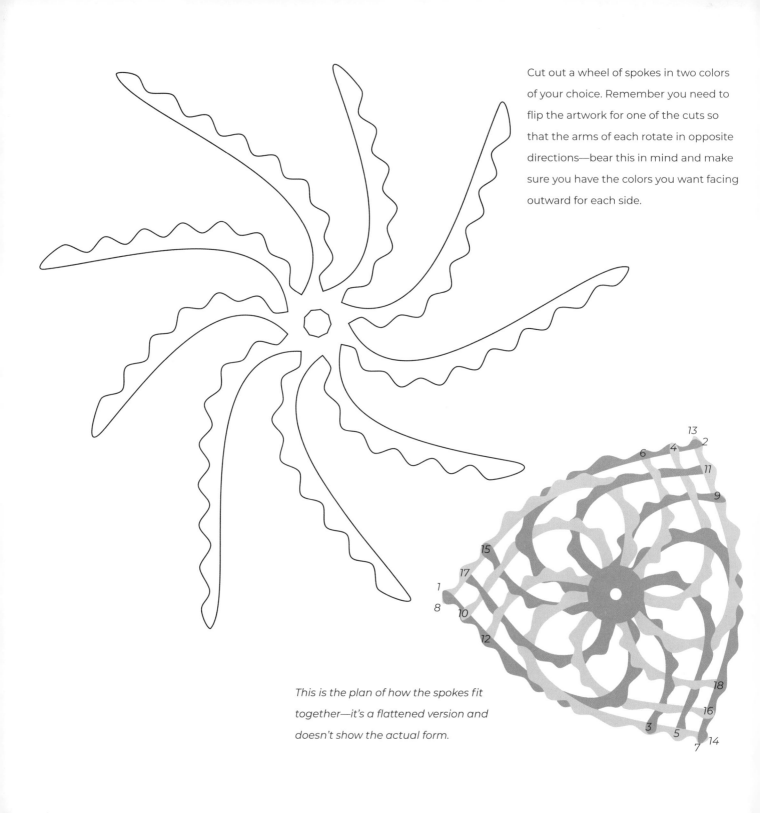

Cut out a wheel of spokes in two colors of your choice. Remember you need to flip the artwork for one of the cuts so that the arms of each rotate in opposite directions—bear this in mind and make sure you have the colors you want facing outward for each side.

This is the plan of how the spokes fit together—it's a flattened version and doesn't show the actual form.

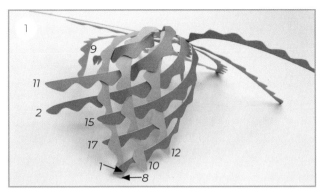

Assembly

Glue the tip of 1 to 8, with 1 on top.

Glue the tip of 17 under the 2nd bump of 8.

Glue the tip of 15 over the 3rd bump of 8.

Weave 10 and 12 over and under 1, 17, and 15 alternately.

Glue tip of 10 over the 2nd bump of 1.

Glue tip of 12 under the 3rd bump of 1.

Weave spokes 2, 11, and 9 through spokes 8, 10, and 12 to start forming petal 2 .

Following the same principles, and taking care to follow the alternating weave pattern:

Glue the tip of 2 to 13, with 2 on top.

Glue the tip of 11 under the 2nd bump of 13.

Glue the tip of 9 on top of the 3rd bump of 13.

Weave spokes 4 and 6 over and under 9 and 11.

Glue tip of 4 over the 2nd bump of 2.

Glue tip of 6 under the 3rd bump of 2.

Weave spokes 3, 5, and 7 through 13, 4, and 6 to start forming petal 3.

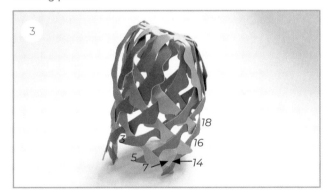

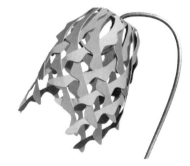

Glue the tip of 7 to 14, with 7 on top.

Glue the tip of 5 under the 2nd bump of 14.

Glue the tip of 3 over the 3rd bump of 14.

Weave the remaining two spokes, 16 and 18, alternately through the woven spokes to end up with the tip of 16 over the 2nd bump of 7, and the tip of 18 under the 3rd bump of 7.

When all the glue is dry, gently roll and squeeze the flower to even up the tension and form a pleasing shape.

Display the flowers by using wire shepherd's hooks, by hanging on threads, or even by using them as lampshades on strings of lights.

"Snowball"

These intricate globes are surprisingly simple to construct and the result is sturdy and fascinating to look at. Try experimenting with different materials —icy vellum, printed stock, sparkling metallics, or even wallpaper.

Assembly

The main trick when assembling the three pieces is to align the curve of one strip next to a straight bit of another strip. This is simple to do for the first two strips, but the third one will need turning.

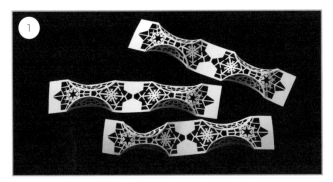

Cut around the black outer lines of the templates on page 79—remember to include the strip marked "Glue."
Lightly score the pink lines then gently crease them.
After creasing the pink lines, fold them back out flat as this makes it easier to assemble the globe.

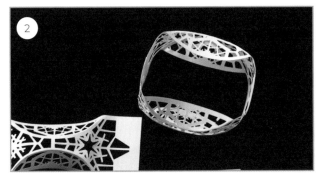

Make a loop out of one piece by gluing in the area marked "Glue."

Make a second loop and tuck it inside the first, at right angles to the first loop.

Make the third loop by threading it behind loop 2, but over loop 1—see photo 4 above. Glue it after threading.
Turn loop three until all the scored half circles are next to the place where the loops meet—check against the photo. Pinch the crease lines to bend the semicircles. This will lock the globe together.

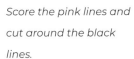

Glue

Cut

Score

Score the pink lines and cut around the black lines.

"Radiolarian"

I am very inspired by the works of Japanese papercutters, in particular Yusuke Oono and his fairytale 360° cut paper books. The books are a collection of single sheets of paper, bound either by wood glue or thread, that enables the sheets to fan out and show off their beautiful forms.

This seemed like the perfect way to explore a form of protozoa called radiolaria. As the name suggests, these have a radial form with a miniscule intricate skeleton made from silica. They grow to become beautiful and elaborate shapes, which are sometimes referred to as "little suns." Their radial arms are outstretched, like a relaxed swimmer's, enabling them to float in ocean currents. The arms also trap food particles on which the radiolaria feed.

For the "Radiolarian" project I made several notches along the spine of each page so as to align precisely when they are stacked. The resulting groove holds an extra thickness of glue, which helps keep it all stuck together. I used PVA glue as it remains flexible when dry, so is ideal for this type of project. While it's drying the sheets are kept pressed tightly together between plywood and clamps. A bookbinding press would be ideal for this, but a flower press is a cheaper alternative.

Right: Radiolarian skeletons gathered from the ocean bottom. The beautiful siliceous skeletons show radial symmetry.

Above left: Ernst Haekel's 1904 drawing of a protozoan that was the inspirational image for my papercut.

In this section we're going to look at a couple of ways to describe form by stacking layers of paper. "Radiolarian" (these pages) stacks the layers on top of each other then splays them out around a central point like a book's spine.

The next example, "Ammonite" (page 84), keeps the layers on top of one another, but pads the space between them to increase the depth.

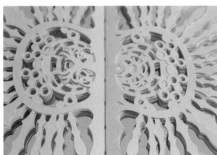

When the notches align they form grooves that will hold a thick band of glue. This makes a strong and flexible binding device.

"Ammonite"

I have a geologist friend with a keen eye for fossils and her home is an absolute delight with many on display and even built into the walls. This piece came from my desire to have one of my very own.

It's possible to find a wide choice of deep frames in home or craft stores and these are perfect for displaying papercutting projects that have some depth to them.

As well as the usual paper cutting equipment, you will need:

- Deep box frame.
- Double-sided foam tape, strips, or squares.
- Thick backing card, at least 250 gsm.
- Paper for the fossil. It is possible to use up to seven colors or tones for the layers.

Step-by-step

Start by checking whether your frame is big enough to contain the piece at the size of the templates (see next pages). If not, you'll need to scan and scale the templates.

Using the templates, see that Line 7, the gray line, is the largest, and that should fit comfortably within the aperture. Remember to note how much the lip of the frame will obscure the edges; take that into account and work within the visible area.

1. Cut the backing sheet to fit in the frame—right to the edges.
2. Cut each of the shapes in your chosen color scheme—plain white is very effective.
3. Start with piece 7. To attach it to the backing sheet, stick

several of the double-sided foam media to the back of piece 7. Keep the foam about 3 mm from the edges. This will start to get fiddly in the finer sections, so the foam will need to be cut into quite small pieces. Doing this will ensure that it is not seen from the front.

4. Keep building up the seven layers in order, 7–1, taking care to slightly rotate each one for the best 3-D effect.

Place in the frame and admire your fossil!

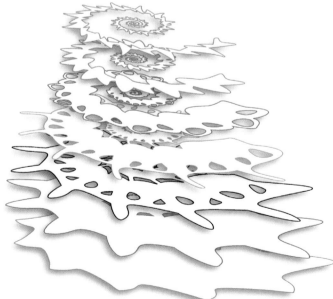

Slice Forms

A paper slice form model is sometimes known as a lattice-style pop. The basic principle is that two sets of cut paper are slotted together in opposing directions to make a 3-D form.

How it works is this: say you have a sliced loaf of bread. You couldn't pick up the whole loaf by picking up just one slice. Imagine there was a second loaf of bread that was sliced in the opposite direction to the first, so that the slices ran down the length of the loaf, rather than across the width. If both sets of slices had slits cut in them so they'd slot together as a lattice grid, then this slotting would lock the two directions of slices together to make a solid shape. Now you could pick up the entire loaf by holding one slice. This construction method is particularly popular in pop-up greeting cards that open to reveal magnificent models such as ships, trees, or gazebos.

To help you become familiar with the principle, I am going to start off by discussing a primitive shape: a torus. This is the geometric term for a doughnut-shaped object. I've chosen it because there is a wealth of research and plenty of example projects based on it. But more than that, the main reason is that some of these projects involve slicing the tori not just in 90° slices, but instead at angles through the rim.

This particular type of section is called a Villarceau Circle, named after mathematician and astronomer Yvon Villarceau (1813–1883). The results are beautiful elegant lattices with off-square divisions. On his Flickr account Professor Yoshinbu Miyamoto has created three very different tori using this principle (shown right).

Looking at the different ways these two approaches can express a form is a great way to train your eye to analyze a shape for breaking down into slice form construction.

In the above model the slices are made through the torus at an angle. The resulting cross section is a Villarceau Circle.

In the top example slices are made through the torus at an angle, while in the bottom one, a grid of slices has been started.

The blue example below shows the approach of taking a simple lattice of 90° slices to make the torus shape.

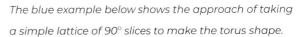

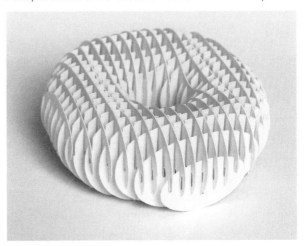

"Sea Urchin"

Radial symmetry is very common in the plant world where the organisms don't have to move about, but is rare in animals. It is found in only two types of creatures: the group Cnidarians, which includes jellyfish, anemones, and corals; and in Echinoderms, which include sea stars, sea urchins, sand dollars, sea cucumbers, and sea lilies.

Sea urchins remind me of a wonderful holiday hopping on and off a small wooden boat between Croatian islands to cycle to deserted beaches. The absolute paradise of warm aquamarine seas but loaded with the peril of putting toes down on one of these spiky creatures. I like the structure of a solid ball contrasting with the fine spines. The space age skeletons they leave behind are also very beautiful and their elegance led me to adapting the Villarceau Circle method to model one.

Using the base model of a torus, I added spines in between the slits so that they wouldn't interfere with the construction process. The spines display a fair bit of artistic license as I wanted to

express some underwater movement with them. Each spine has a slightly different curve to it, and as the pieces are assembled in no particular order, this will throw a random element into the mix.

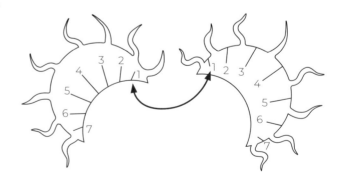

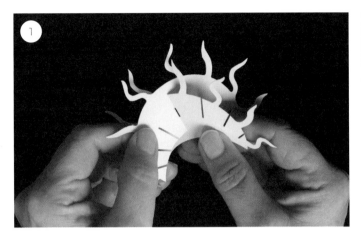

When assembling the form, a piece with slits on the outer curve always slots into a piece with slits on the inner curve. They will always attach at the same numbered slit. Here, both are slotted together at slit 3.

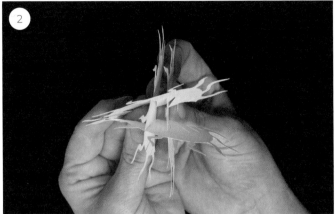

Another two pieces have been added, joining the original two at slit 4 on the left and right, before slotting with each other at slit 5.

Yet further pieces are added and the lattice that's being formed is becoming clearer to see.

"Mistletoe Ball"

This beautiful ball of mistletoe has at its base a geometrical form called a platonic solid. Platonic solids are formed from identical modules. In this case, an equilateral triangle forms the base shape that can be assembled in sets.

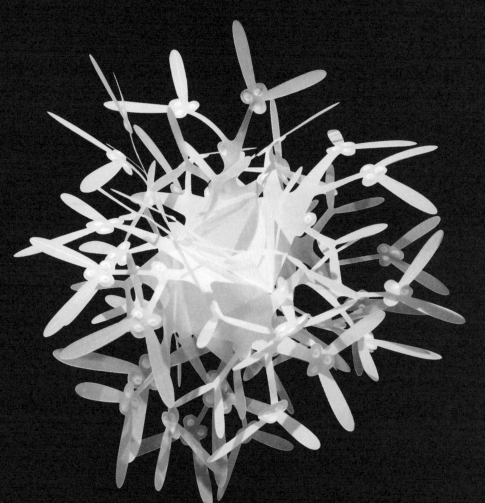

This shape is formed from sets of triangles stuck together along the fold lines. The number of faces created depends on the number of triangles. Three triangles stuck together create a tetrahedron, four triangles an octahedron, and five triangles an icosahedron.

In this project the form grows out from the triangles to make a mistletoe ball.

The example shown here is made in vellum and, instead of cutting out circles for the berries, they have been left solid and embossed (see page 11 for the technique). Make the ball large out of Tyvek or card to hang above your front door, or small and glittery for the Christmas tree. The ball can also be assembled without glue, in which case, halve the score line that forms the triangle and make a cut instead; then the pieces will slot together.

Cut out four templates of each.

Score and fold the pink lines.

Cut around the black lines.

Cut

Score

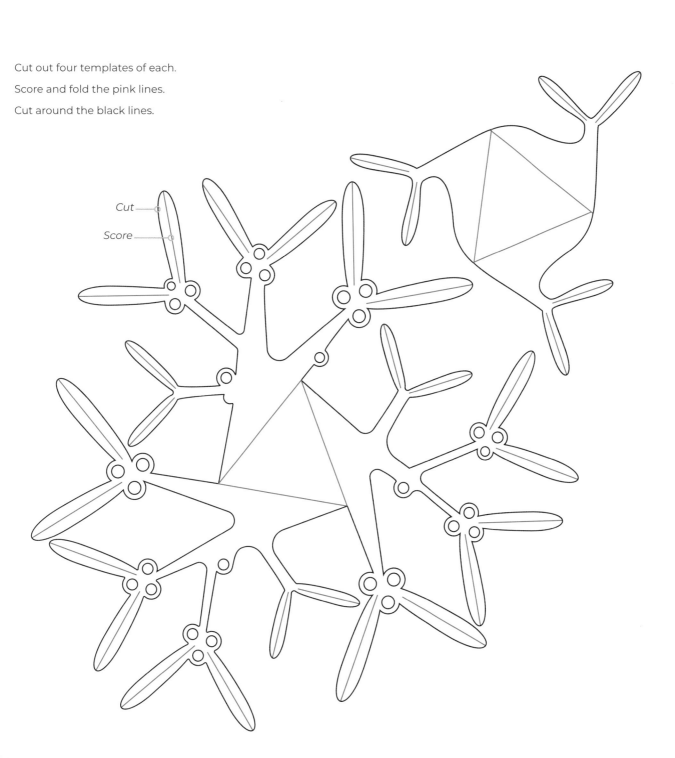

Step-by-step

Cut out four of each type of template. You will need two of each type for each half of the octahedron. Score, crease, and fold as shown on the diagram on page 93.

Glue a larger part to a smaller part, carefully gluing only along the fold line. Leave to dry.

Repeat, then make a pyramid with the two sets of glued parts. Glue along the seam that joins the two sets and leave to dry. Flip it over and smear the inside of the pyramid with glue. Set aside to dry.

When dry, bend and shape the leaves to form a rounded shape.

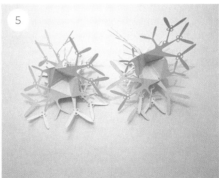

Repeat to make a second pyramid.

Glue the two pyramids to each other, making sure you always match a larger part to a smaller part. Leave to dry.

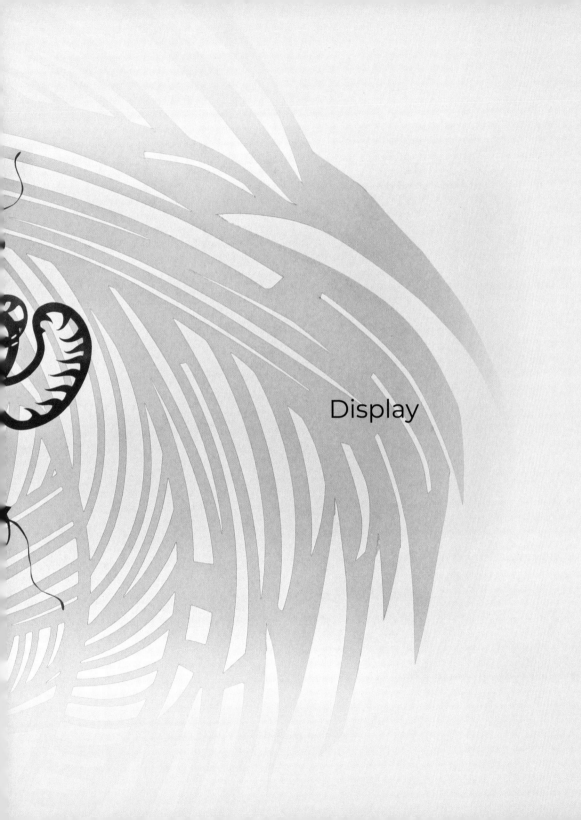

Display

Display

Now let's turn to works where the properties of material, their position, transparency, and their interaction with lighting are fundamental to the papercut.

In previous chapters, I showed how to use paper to block light in the "Sleeping Beauty" lampshade, and how to enjoy the light reflected off mirror card being picked up and transmitted by vellum in "Lichen Rosettes." The works in this section seek to express or control the display aspects more by both exploiting materials and environment.

The "UV Jellyfish" project presents a number of very interesting structural techniques, where the nature of the light is completely different from ordinary everyday light. The combination of strange structures and ethereal lighting makes for a very deliberately other-worldly display.

In the first of the frieze projects, "UV Jellyfish" (page 100), there are three levels of reflectivity presented in a conventional assemblage.

The second project, "Undersea Frieze" (page 102), encourages exploration in the positioning of opaque and translucent materials. In this multi-positional project elements can either reflect light, or block it and become silhouettes of shadow. This effect will depend on their display position in relation to the available light source. For the third project, "Diatoms" (page 124), we have two levels of reflectivity but multi-positional aspects.

In the lightboxes pages we look at fixed light sources that are designed alongside the cut work to bring out specific qualities in the cut paper. These are displays where the lighting environment is fixed and controlled. How materials respond to light after deliberate pressure or breaking down of their surface is also considered.

Display

"UV Jellyfish"

This piece uses ultraviolet, or UV, light. The bottom left photograph shows the jellyfish in normal lighting, and in the image at bottom right it appears ethereal when illuminated with black light.

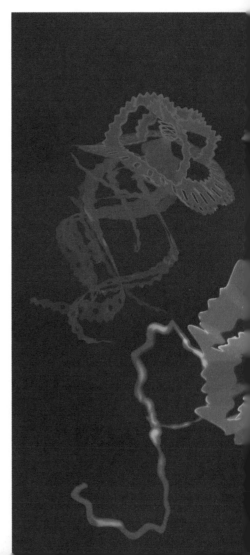

Violet is the furthest point on one end of the spectrum that's visible to humans, and radiation on the spectrum beyond this is named ultraviolet. UV lamps are sometimes called black lights and they cause this radiation to glow, or fluoresce, so we can see it. Importantly, they don't give out any other visible light to spoil the effect.

In 1992 I took a wonderful road trip from San Francisco down Highway 1 and stopped off at Monterey. At the awe-inspiring Monterey Bay Aquarium I was lucky enough to catch the temporary exhibition *Planet of the Jellies*. Huge tanks of jellyfish were lit with UV light to fascinating effect.

I often think about the exhibition, especially as when I'm out walking on the estuary here at home, stranded jellyfish are a common sight. I have been playing with the idea of creating something similar ever since in the form of party and set decorations.

These smaller-scale jellyfish are made out of vellum and suspended with fine black thread. Vellum is a good paper to use as it carries some of the light through it, emitting a gentle glow, but keeps its translucent quality. For the parts that appear as though lit up, the creatures are drawn on with UV pen—the colorless kind you mark property with. Fluorescent highlighters work well and glow true to the color of their packaging. Fluorescent papers are also available to cut from and can be sourced from stationery and craft retailers.

For the form of the creatures, I drew on the teachings of Josef Albers. Albers taught a course in paper study at the Bauhaus in Dassau from 1927 to 1928. The drawing out of spiraling shapes of such immense volume and grace from a flat sheet of paper seems almost magical.

Black lights are easily sourced and these days many are adapted to be safe for longterm exposure. They come as bulbs for standard domestic light fittings and as battery powered lamps for remote installations. For this piece I used plug-in LED strips, which are really versatile. They can be tucked behind baffles and stuck into tiny corners, as well as being used as an array to flood an area with light. They make a great starting point for your own experiments with UV decorating and display projects.

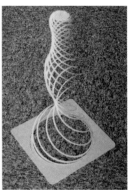

Right: Bauhaus Spiral experiment as inspired by Josef Albers.

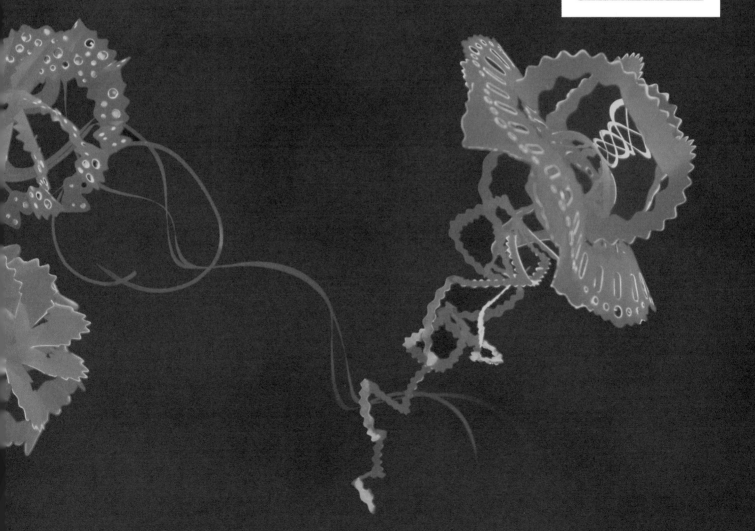

Lightboxes

Lightboxes offer a controlled environment that provides light to bring out specific aspects of your papercut project. They can be constructed without depth so that in effect the back piece of a regular picture is illuminated, or have varying degrees of depth so that there is interplay between the layers.

The availability and affordability of LEDs with their cool operating temperature and the option of being battery-powered makes them a versatile resource. They are also available with color-changing properties, which has the potential of adding another aspect to the work.

The subject matter

Many people have been drawn to the beautiful shapes of diatoms and have been inspired to make intricate patterns from arrangements of whole diatoms. The cyanotype above dates from the 1870s and modern day examples can be seen in the work of Klaus Kemp.

Diatoms are microalgae found in both soil and water all over the world and generate about 20% of our planet's oxygen each year. These microscopic single-celled organisms display the most elegant symmetry, which can be radial, reflection, or rotational, and can then take the shape of ellipses, fans, and stars.

Each diatom is surrounded by a cell wall of silica. This glassy case interacts with light rays giving the diatoms the appearance of changing body color, and causing them to be referred to as jewels of the sea or living opals.

Right: A group of fossil diatoms collected from Bori, Hungary, in September 1895 and viewed under the light microscope using differential interference contrast.

This cyanotype physiogram is attributed to Austrian botanist Julius Wiesner (1838–1916). It is an arrangement of plankton skeletons seen through the microscope, and dates from the 1870s.

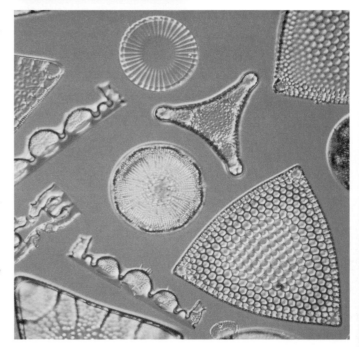

"Diatoms"

The piece on the previous spread is inspired by looking at diatoms through a microscope. It is an example of a lightbox that is cube-shaped, which gives a lot of depth so there is room to think about the space between, and interplay of, materials.

The fascinating diatoms on the previous spread are the subject matter for this build, but I also wanted to capture that feeling of looking through a microscope. When you look through the eyepiece of a microscope not everything is visible at a glance—you have to look around and sometimes alter the focus. I have tried to replicate this feeling by having a small aperture at the front of the lightbox. You have to peer around at the inside through this hole and the decreasing concentric circles that hold the cuts in position deliberately restrict your view. I like the feeling that really tiny organisms are now big and close to your face.

The box was sourced from a well known international furnishing store and is lit by a bank of LEDs positioned onto the back panel. They comprise two sets of standard strips in warm white that you can find in DIY stores. A hole was drilled in the rear panel for the cord to come out.

It is also possible to mount your lights around the edges of your box or frame and have them hidden by the first layer of paper. Having lights around the edges is a good solution for narrow boxes as they are already hidden and so won't need diffusing. This box has too much depth and too many overlaping layers for that to be practical, as the light needs to shine strongly here through all the layers so they can all be seen.

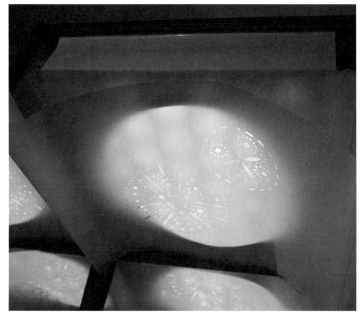

If your light source is visible from the viewing angle then the next thing to consider is whether you want to soften the appearance of those lights and, if so, how to diffuse them. Vellum makes for an excellent diffuser and the farther away it is from the lights the more diffused they will be. Interestingly, two layers of vellum that aren't touching will diffuse lights very effectively, even if they are in close proximity both to each other and the light source. The eventual spacing is determined by moving the two sheets of vellum around with the lights switched on until the desired effect is achieved and then marking the positions.

As well as diffusing the light sources, I wanted to give the impression of a narrow depth of field. I found that by making an opaque frame with a circular aperture for one of the sheets, then curving the sheet of vellum diffuser in front of it, I could replicate a falloff of focus. You can see that in the middle of the curve where the two layers are closest, the frame at the back is in sharp focus. As the sheet of vellum curves away, the frame's appearance blurs out.

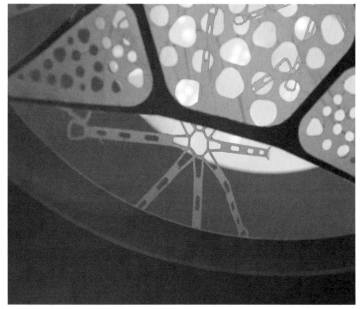

The papers used are vellum and white card—note how the translucence of the vellum makes it appear lit up in places. In some areas the vellum has been scrunched; where this has happened the stress forces in the material has made it go white and opaque. The material is no longer translucent in these areas and has an effect of marbled shadow.

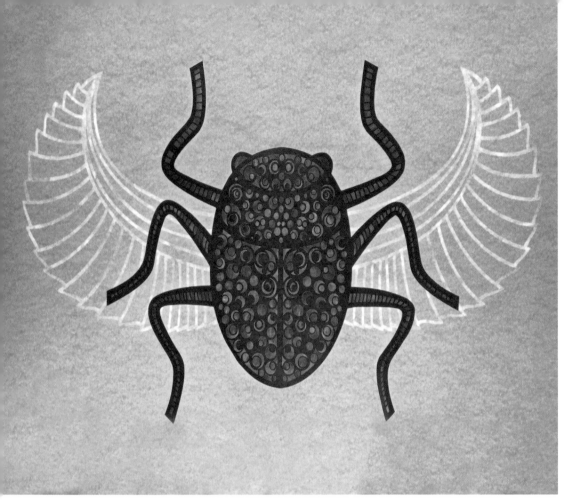

Back-lighting: Art Deco "Scarab"

Next in this section we'll be looking at back-lighting in a shadow box. This can incorporate a lot of depth and, by using layers and different densities of paper, explore shadow and focus. But here, we're paring it right back and exploring the effect of back-lighting within the sheet of paper itself.

This piece has at its roots the stunning Egyptian influenced Art Nouveau and Art Deco style jewelery. Egyptian style was a huge influence in art and architecture as early as 1798, when Napoleon Bonaparte launched his campaign into Egypt and the area was first mapped in detail. The discovery of the tomb of Tutankhamen in 1922 brought about a revival of Egyptian style on a huge scale. The popular scarab beetle motif combined with the geometric stylization of Art Deco is a perfect combination of subjects.

Carving the paper for transparency

To make paper, fibers are soaked and pounded to make a kind of soup called pulp. This wet pulp is sometimes passed between hot rollers to both dry the pulp and to give the paper a final finished surface. A hot-rolled finish is crisp and smooth, and with the thicker weights of paper and card, it's possible to dig back in to expose the rougher pulp inside.

To achieve this, rather than cutting straight through, the sheet is scored. Areas between the scored lines are then dug out and peeled. This leads to an interesting play between the smooth finished surface and the pulpy inner content that now has a look of suede about it. The juxtaposition of textures is really pleasing in itself, but another element can be added with lighting.

The "Scarab" piece was assembled from two sheets of paper. The top piece of paper has the body of the scarab beetle peeled into it on the upper surface so that texture is always visible. The piece underneath holds the work on the wings. As the two sheets are the same size, there is no clue as to the existence of the wings until the light is switched on.

The light that works the wings also illuminates the carved away areas in the beetle. While a similar effect could be made by overlaying two sheets of thinner paper, with one of them having areas completely cut away, this technique makes for variation in the brightness as fewer or more layers of pulp are removed. A gradient of emphasis can also be made by careful ripping and removal of the pulp to varying depths.

"Undersea Frieze"

Here we have all the elements to make this enchanting "Undersea Frieze" three very different ways.

The first version is a straight flat assembly. The second explores folding triangles, which can be positioned in many ways to interesting effect. And the third has only vertical folds.

Frieze 1

This is a simple, free-style frieze that is a great way to tune in to the shapes used in the more complex versions. Experiment with combinations of colors and textures before moving on to the more complex Friezes 2 and 3.

In the example on the left, the frieze has been made up to a 12 x 14 inch size. The same card has been used for both the swirls and the background, providing interest while still keeping the composition light. A mid-sheen gunmetal card provides a textural bridge between the matte base card and the glitter card of the top details.

Step-by-step

1. From Templates F and G (pages 119–120), cut the blue and orange shapes in your chosen material.

2. Decorate with elements from templates A to E (pages 114–118), and explore compositions and changes of scale, texture, reflectivity, and color.

Frieze 2

This is a folding, multi-position version that's as much a papercutting toy as decoration.

A range of some of the positions the frieze can be twisted and folded into—it can also, of course, be displayed simply as a long strip.

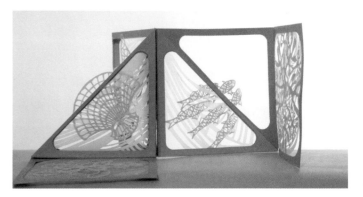

Step-by-step

1. From templates I and J (pages 122–123) cut the lines in the card, once with the tab, once without.
   Cut two shapes in template H (without the tab, page 121), and cut L (page 125) four times in translucent material.

2. From template K (page 124) cut the lines in the card four times and score the pink lines. Two of the pieces need to be flipped to run in the opposite direction, but the tab must remain on the left.

Template I x 1

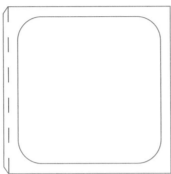
Template J x 1

Template H x 2

Template L x 4

3. Line up the pieces cut from card in the order shown here. The first piece won't have a tab and the last one will. Score the pink lines and bend them in both directions.

4. Glue the tab of each card to the card to its left.

5. Stick the vellum over the windows formed in the card as shown.

6. Once assembled, decorate with pieces from templates A to E (pages 114–118).

Template K x 4

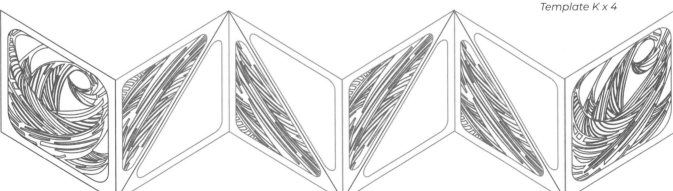

Frieze 3

Folding zigzag version

A dramatic black background with deep glitter card elements has been chosen for this version. It looks great folded to an open zigzag shape running along a mantelpiece or shelf.

Step-by-step

1. From template H (page 121) cut the card out, once with a tab and once without.

2. From templates M and N (pages 126–127) cut two cards and score the pink lines.

Template H x 1

Template H x 1

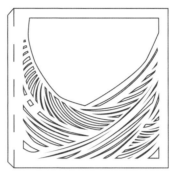
Template M x 2

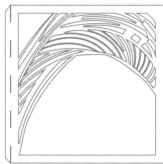
Template N x 2

3. Line the pieces cut from card in the order shown above.
   The first piece won't have a tab and the last one will.
   Score the pink lines and bend them in both directions.

4. Glue the tab of each card to the card on its left.

5. Once assembled, decorate with pieces from Templates A to E (pages 114–118).

Center of
Brittlestar

Brittlestar

Template A

Wrack

Template B

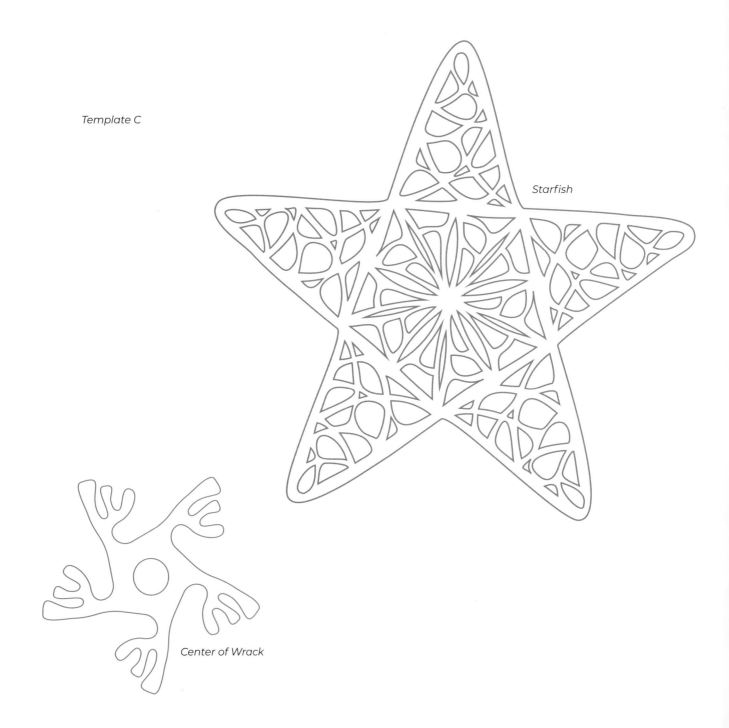

Template C

Starfish

Center of Wrack

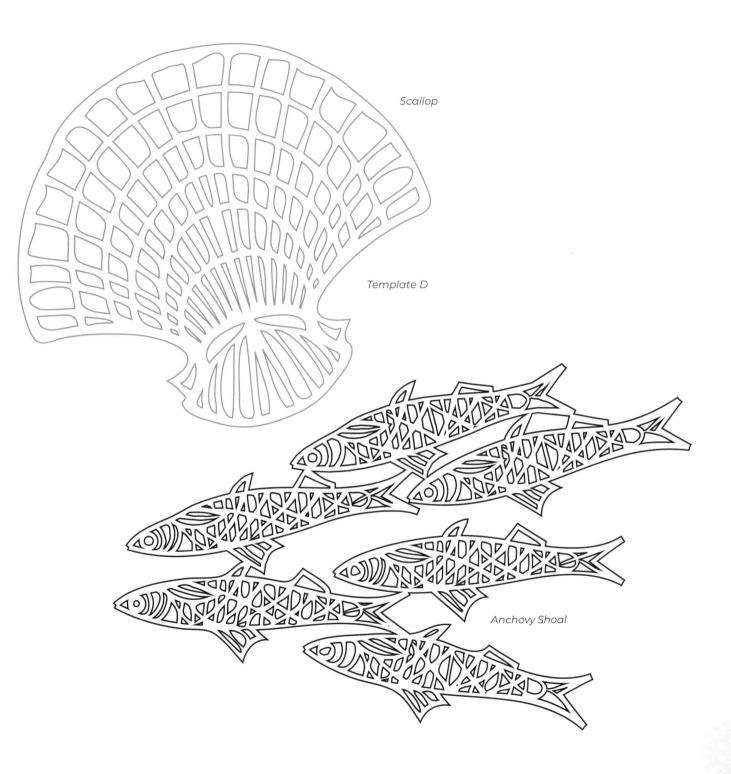

Scallop

Template D

Anchovy Shoal

Template E

Small Scollop

Seahorse

Template F

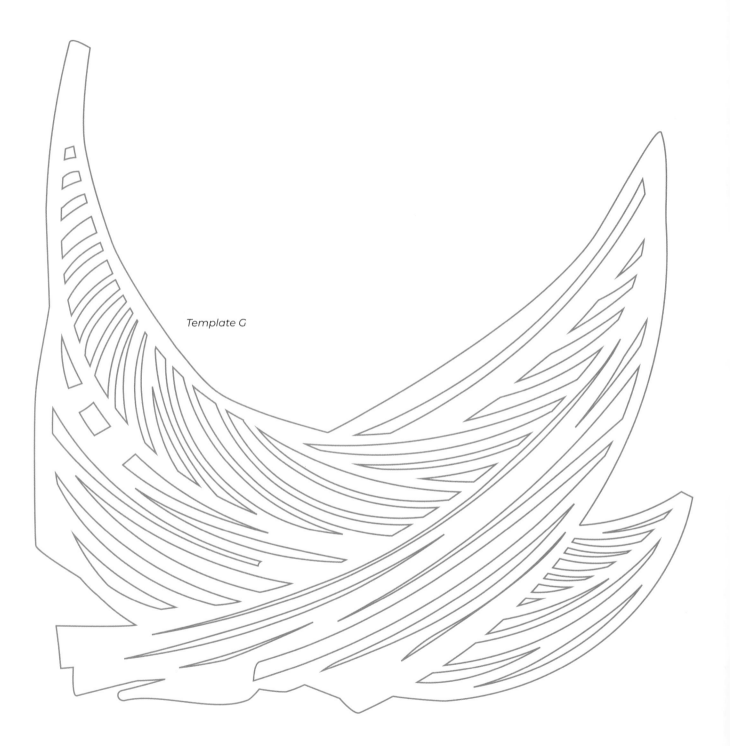

Template G

Template H

Template I

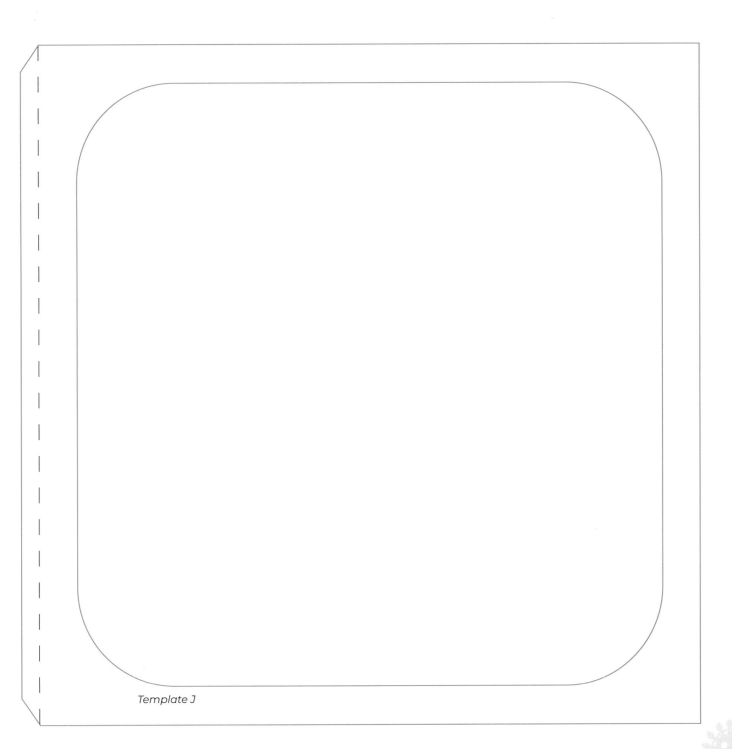

Template J

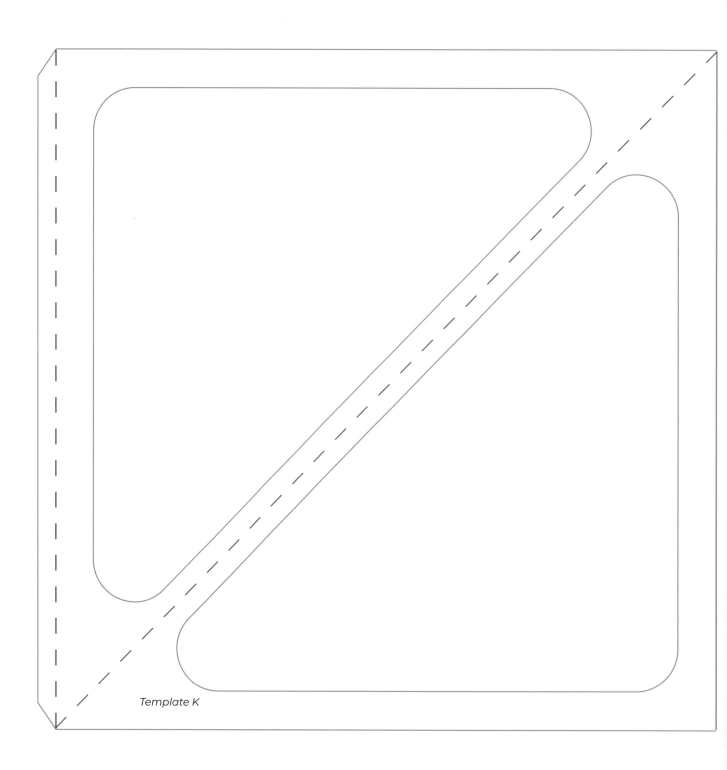

Template K

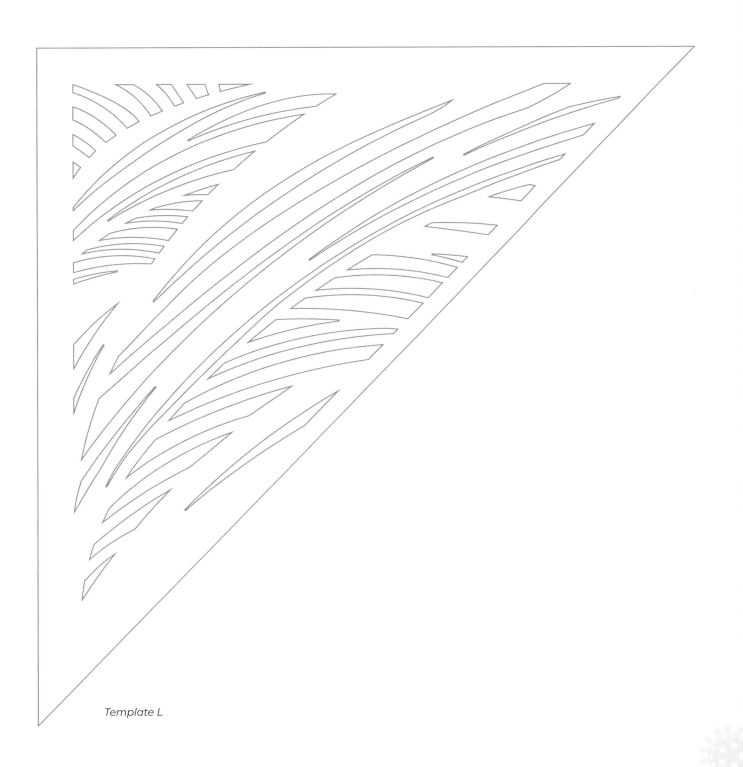

Template L

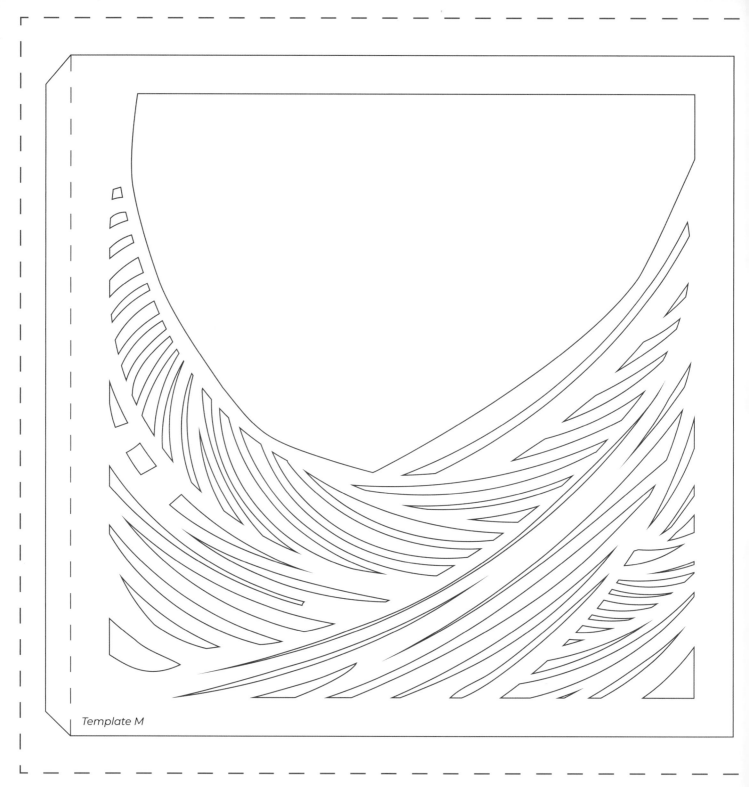

Template M

Template N

Further Reading

Wade, David. *Symmetry: The Ordering Principle,* Wooden Books, 2006.

Wade, David. *Li: Dynamic Form in Nature* (Mathemagical Ancient Wizdom), Wooden Books, 2007.

Schepper, Anna and Lene. *The Art of Paper Weaving: 46 Colorful, Dimensional Projects*, Quarry Books, 2015.

Hargittai, István and Hargittai, Magdolna. *Symmetry: A Unifying Concept*, Random House, 1996.

Jackson, Paul. *Cut and Fold Techniques for Promotional Materials*, Laurence King Publishing, 2013.

Jackson, Paul. *Cut and Fold Techniques for Pop-Up Designs*, Laurence King Publishing, 2014.

Penrose, Roger. *Altair Design: Penrose Tilings*, Wooden Books, 2013.

http://algorithmicbotany.org

pp. 26-27: The theory behind the murmurations of starlings: https://warwick.ac.uk/newsandevents/pressreleases/the_mystery_behind

pp. 116-117: The diatom arrangements of Klaus Kemp, www.diatoms.co.uk

Further Watching

pp. 116-117: *The Beauty of Diatoms: Perspectives on Ocean Science*, University of California Television (UCTV).

pp. 78-79: Yusuke Oono, Making of a 360° book: https://www.youtube.com/watch?v=jPea1Z1eQ6s

Acknowledgments

Studio photography: Adrienne Roisin

P. 7 Gregory Phillips | Wikimedia, p. 8 AjayTvm | Shutterstock, p. 21 bilwissedition Ltd & Co KG | Alamy Stock Photo, p. 24 The Picture Art Collection | Alamy Stock Photo, p. 27 redsnapper | Alamy Stock Photo, p. 43 Anton Starikov | Alamy Stock Photo, p. 48 Nguyen Tran | Pexels, p. 58 Dariusz Szwangruber | Dreamstime.com, p. 70 Ganna Albetova | Alamy Stock Photo, p. 80 Scott Camazine | Alamy Stock Photo, p. 81 Wim Van Egomond | Science Photo Library, p. 88 Miyamoto Yakamoto | Flickr, p. 90 Greg Amptman | Shutterstock, p. 101 top Miyamoto Yakamoto | Flickr, p. 102 top age fotostock | Alamy Stock Photo, bottom The Natural History Museum | Alamy Photo Library.

Location of garland photograph on p. 69: The Mirror Room, one of the Portmeirion Hotel's sumptuous wedding locations. https://portmeirion.wales

For endless inspiration:
The works of Angie Lewin and Mike Tanis.
Mackintosh Watercolours, Roger Billcliffe, Cameron Books, 1978.
The Grammar of Ornament, Owen Jones, Day and Sons, 1856. Available in many facsimile editions.
Kunstformen der Natur (Art Forms of Nature), Ernst Haeckel, 1904. Available in many facsimile editions.
The Math Book, Clifford A. Pickover, Sterling Publishing, 2009.
Guy Petzall at Ullagami, www.ullagami.com

For geological fact checking, my pal Nikki Charlton.

For constant sustenance, bath-running, encouragement, inspiration, technical setup, idea-batting . . . but most of all, love, my thanks to my wonderful husband, Kevin.